CHAT AND SHARE!

TOPIC STARTERS FOR TODAY'S STUDENTS

Diane H. Nagatomo

JN033981

KINSEIDO

Kinseido Publishing Co., Ltd.

3-21 Kanda Jimbo-cho, Chiyoda-ku,
Tokyo 101-0051, Japan

First published 2020 by Kinseido Publishing Co., Ltd.

Cover design	Takayuki Minegishi
Text design	Shigoka Co., Ltd.
Illustrations	Chiaki Tagami

音声ファイル無料ダウンロード

http://www.kinsei-do.co.jp/download/4106

この教科書で 🎧 DL 00 の表示がある箇所の音声は、上記 URL または QR コードにて無料でダウンロードできます。自習用音声としてご活用ください。

- ▶ PC からのダウンロードをお勧めします。スマートフォンなどでダウンロードされる場合は、ダウンロード前に「解凍アプリ」をインストールしてください。
- ▶ URL は、検索ボックスではなくアドレスバー (URL 表示欄) に入力してください。
- ▶ お使いのネットワーク環境によっては、ダウンロードできない場合があります。

🔘 CD 00　左記の表示がある箇所の音声は、教室用 CD (Class Audio CD) に収録されています。

Preface

Welcome to **_Chat and Share!_** _Topic Starters for Today's Students._ In this four-skills book, students will improve their basic conversational skills while following the lives of six college students in Japan. Mai and Yuya (from Japan) share their ideas, hopes, and dreams with four foreign students: Sophie (from the US), Jack (from Australia), Kaira (from India) and Angelo (from the Philippines). In 15 chapters, these characters will discuss topics that are of interest to college students all over the world, ranging from free time activities, food, and fashion to Japanese culture, the environment, and modern families. This provides a springboard for students to start expressing their own ideas on these topics. Most students want to talk about important things, but they often lack the language skills that enable them to do so in English. This textbook is aimed at lower-level students (CEFR A1 and A2). Approximately 85% of the vocabulary is at K-1 on AWL (Academic Word List) and the grammar structures are fairly simple. Even students who lack confidence or who have fallen behind in their English studies should be able to start talking immediately, and before they know it, they will be able to have real conversations in English. English is not just a "subject" to study in school, but it is a language spoken by millions of people in the world. This book aims to motivate students and to show them that it is never too late to master English!

Many thanks to Victoria Yoshimura and to Suzanne Kamata for providing photos for Chapters 8 and 14. And most importantly, I would like to thank Michi Tsutahara for her keen eye for details and her wonderful editing skills. This book would not have been possible without her and I owe her a great deal of gratitude.

Finally, here is an important message for all students: Remember, you can speak English if you learn the basics and if you keep on trying. Follow your dream and you will find that nothing is impossible!

Breaking the Ice

This warm-up exercise gets you to start thinking about the topic. You will be asked to give your own answers to some simple questions. Later, you will put your thoughts and opinions to use!

Getting the Topic

Vocabulary Matching

You can expand your vocabulary by matching key words from the reading with English definitions.

Reading

The short readings will introduce you to perspectives of culture, fashion, travel, family, lifestyles and diversity that you might not have considered before. The vocabulary and grammar is easy, so you should be able to read most of them easily without a dictionary.

True or False

You can check your understanding of the reading by answering the true-false questions.

Speaking Up

Conversation A

Conversation A ❶ provides reading, listening, and speaking practice. The natural conversations are like those carried out by college students everywhere. You will listen to the characters' dialogs, fill in some missing information, and then practice with your friends.

Then in ❷, you will take the words and expressions from the previous section to create and practice your own mini conversations. This will help you build confidence to make your own original conversations on various topics.

Conversation B

Conversation B provides more reading, listening and speaking practice. You will complete two key sentences by listening to the speaker. Here's a hint: the number of words you will need is given at the end of each sentence. These sentences are useful in everyday conversations. They will help you express your own opinion. Then, you will put to use all the expressions you have learned so far in the chapter to create your own conversations.

Expressing Yourself

⤹ Your Opinion

This section provides you with the opportunity to express your own opinions. Through guided exercises, you will learn how to support your opinion with an example or a reason.

⤹ Writing

Each chapter has a different writing task that is very practical. You will fill out an application, send an email, write an online review, and send text messages. These simple exercises reflect many kinds of writing you will have to do in the real world.

Character Profiles

Yuya (Japan)
- Freshman majoring in Economics
- A little quiet, but a really nice guy
- Likes computers and watching YouTube

Mai (Japan)
- Sophomore majoring in Sociology
- Head of the International Student Association
- Loves English and meeting new people

Sophie (the US)
- Sophomore majoring in Japanese
- Organized and ambitious
- Loves books and is interested in Japanese literature

Jack (Australia)
- Junior majoring in Hospitality Management
- Outgoing and adventurous
- Loves sports and eating

Angelo (the Philippines)
- Junior majoring in Law
- Likes to try new things
- Good at cooking and using computers

Kaira (India)
- Junior majoring in Business
- Loves traveling
- Crazy about Japanese pop culture

Table of Contents

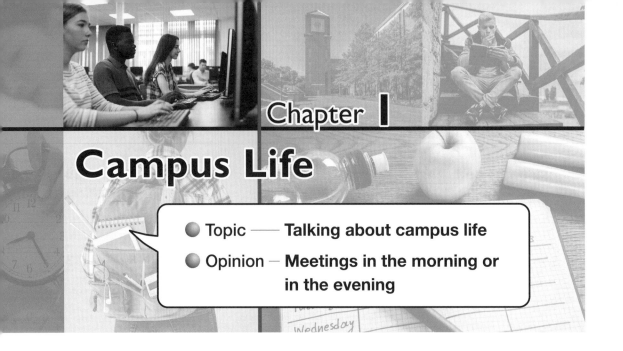

Chapter 1

Campus Life

- Topic —— **Talking about campus life**
- Opinion — **Meetings in the morning or in the evening**

Breaking the Ice

Fill in the blanks with your information, and then practice asking and answering the questions with your partner. DL 02 CD1-02

1. What time do you wake up every day?

　—I wake up at _____ every day.

2. How long does it take you to get ready in the morning?

　—It takes me about _____.

3. Do you spend more time studying or hanging out with friends?

　—I spend more time _____.

4. Do you prefer studying in the morning or at night?

　—I prefer studying _____.

Getting the Topic

Vocabulary Matching Match each word or expression with its meaning.

1. manage time　·

2. recommend　·

3. submit　·

4. practical　·

5. pack　·

　· **a.** to turn in

　· **b.** to put things into a bag

　· **c.** to decide what to do and when to do it

　· **d.** to advise

　· **e.** useful and helpful

How busy are you?

Learning how to manage time is important. Experts recommend planning ahead and dividing days into blocks of time. It is important to not only schedule time for school, part-time jobs, and study, but also for meeting friends, exercising, and even playing video games. 5

Adults often tell teenagers what to do and when to do it. But college students must learn how to manage time themselves. They must wake up, 10 go to class, and submit assignments on time. Unfortunately, this is difficult for many students to do.

Here are two practical tips that can help you. Prepare everything you need for school the night before. Pack your bag and decide what you will wear. By doing these things, you can save a lot of time in the morning. 15 Another useful tip is using a timer. Set it for twenty minutes and focus on a task that must be done. Don't check your phone! You can do a lot in twenty minutes. After that, take a five-minute break. Soon the job will be finished and you can spend time on things you like.

True or False | Answer if the statement is true or false.

1. It is a good idea to make a schedule for work, study, and leisure. [T / F]
2. College students find it easy to manage time. [T / F]
3. Checking your phone often can help you get a lot done. [T / F]
4. It is good to focus on a task for twenty minutes. [T / F]

Speaking Up

Conversation A Mai and Yuya like to practice English with each other. Here, they are talking about after-school activities.

❶ Listen to their conversation and fill in the blanks. Next, practice it with your partner. 🎧 DL 04 💿 CD1-04

Mai: What do you do ¹_____ school, Yuya?

Yuya: I usually study in the library. Then I ²_____ go home or go to my part-time job.

Mai: Wow. I ³_____ you're a loner.

Yuya: I'd like to make new friends, but to tell the ⁴_____, I'm a ⁵_____ shy.

Mai: You should ⁶_____ us at the International Student Association.

Yuya: What do you do there?

Mai: We have discussions about ⁷_____ cultures. We visit some interesting ⁸_____ in Tokyo. We have parties. It's a lot of fun! Why don't you come to our next ⁹_____?

Yuya: Maybe I will. It sounds interesting. I want to study abroad next year, so a club ¹⁰_____ that might be good for me.

▶ Now list the International Student Association's activities.

- have discussions about ( )
- visit some ( ) in Tokyo
- have ( )

❷ Using the expressions you have learned so far, fill in the blanks and then practice these three mini-conversations with your partner.

1. A: What do you do _____ school?

   B: I usually _____ home, but today I'm going to do some shopping.

2. A: You want to _____ new friends? OK, you _____ join our English club.

   B: What do you do there?

3. A: _____ don't you come to our club meeting this Friday?

   B: I think I _____. It sounds _____!

Conversation B The members of the International Student Association are introducing themselves to Yuya.

❶ Listen to their conversation and complete the two key sentences.

Conversation 🎧 DL 05 ◎ CD1-05 **Key Sentences** 🎧 DL 06 ◎ CD1-06

Mai: Before we start our meeting, let's welcome Yuya. Tell him where you're from and say one interesting thing about yourself.

Jack: I'm from Sydney. I like sports and eating!

Sophie: I'm from the U.S. I want to be a novelist.

Kaira: I'm from India. I'm crazy about Japanese manga!

Angelo: I'm from the Philippines. I'm majoring in law.

Yuya: Nice to meet you all! I'm from Japan and I want to study abroad someday.

Mai: 🔑1 Yuya, we _____

_____ (9 words)

at 5:00.

Yuya: Oh. I work every Wednesday evening.

Sophie: 🔑2 Why don't _____ (7)?

Jack: In the morning? Before nine? You can't be serious!

❷ Take turns being A, B, and C and practice this conversation with two friends. You can choose expressions from the hints or think of your own.

A: Before we start our meeting, please introduce yourself to name .

B: I'm name . I'm from hometown . I'm majoring in a , and I'm crazy about b !

C: Nice to meet you, name . My major is a .

B: Nice to meet you too, name .

C: How often do you have meetings?

A: We usually meet c .

Hints

- **a** literature / management / economics / physics / computer science
- **b** video games / Italian food / American TV dramas / photography
- **c** once a month / every other day / every day except Tuesdays and Sundays

Expressing Yourself

Your Opinion Express your own view by answering the following question. Review the key sentences you learned on the previous page, if you like.

❓ **Question**

> Which would you prefer, having club meetings in the morning, afternoon, or evening?

—I prefer _____ because _____

_____

—I don't want to _____ because _____

_____

Writing a Self-introduction Imagine you want to join the International Student Association. Fill out this application form and write a short paragraph about yourself.

▶ First, fill out the application form.

International Student Association Application Form		
· Name	[	]
· Nickname	[	]
· Major	[	]
· Interests	[	]
· How many classes?	[	]
· Busiest day of the week	[	]

▶ Next, complete this short paragraph by filling in your own information.

● *About Me* ●

My name is _____. *Everyone calls me* _____.
I'm majoring in _____.
My interests are _____ *and* _____.
I have _____ *classes. The busiest day of the week for me is* _____.

12

Chapter 2

Weekends

- ● Topic —— **Talking about weekends**
- ● Opinion — **Stay home or go out**

Breaking the Ice

Fill in the blanks with your information, and then practice asking and answering the questions with your partner.　🎧 DL 07　◎ CD1-07

1. Which do you like better, weekends or weekdays?
   —I like _____ better.
2. When do you study more, on weekends or on weekdays?
   —I study more _____ .
3. Which do you like better, singing karaoke or going hiking?
   —I like _____ better.
4. Which would you prefer, a difficult job with a high salary or an easier job with an average salary?
   —I'd prefer _____ .

Getting the Topic

Vocabulary Matching Match each word or expression with its meaning.

1. employees　　　·　　　· **a.** spend several days or more away from work
2. take a vacation　·　　　· **b.** repeated one after another
3. days off　　　　·　　　· **c.** people you work with
4. in a row　　　　·　　　· **d.** time that you don't have to work
5. colleagues　　　·　　　· **e.** people who work in a company

Who has the most days off?

DL 08 CD1-08

Workers in Sweden have more days off than workers in most other countries. They have 41 paid vacation days. There are public holidays throughout the year and workers often have several weeks of vacation in the summer as well. Employees can also take personal days off if they need to attend a funeral or move to a different house. Despite these long holidays, Sweden has a strong economy. Swedish people feel that taking vacations can help them be more productive at work.

Japanese workers have fewer days off than workers in any other developed country. There are national holidays, but few people take long vacations. In fact, a recent survey showed that Japanese employees use less than 50% of their paid annual vacation time, and they rarely take many days off in a row. The main reason for this is they feel guilty if they are away from the office. They do not want to add to their colleagues' workloads. But nowadays, many job-hunting students in Japan prefer seeking jobs in companies that offer more paid vacation time. Will this change the future of Japanese companies and the Japanese economy?

5

10

15

20

True or False Answer if the statement is true or false.

1. People in Sweden have more days off than most other countries.   [T / F]

2. The Swedish economy is weak because workers take long vacations. [T / F]

3. Japanese workers have fewer holidays than workers in any other developed country.   [T / F]

4. Most Japanese employees use all of their vacation days.   [T / F]

Speaking Up

Conversation A Yuya and Kaira are making plans for the evening.

❶ Listen to their conversation and fill in the blanks. Next, practice it with your partner. 🎧 DL 09 💿 CD1-09

Yuya: The weekend is almost here. I'm so happy.

Kaira: Me, too. Do you ¹_____ ²_____ go to karaoke after school?

Yuya: I can't. I'm ³_____ my brother. He usually ⁴_____
⁵_____ every day, but he's ⁶_____ a day off today.

Kaira: What are you guys going to do?

Yuya: We're going to see a movie in the afternoon and have dinner in the
evening. Do you ⁷_____ to come?

Kaira: Oh. I have a Japanese class ⁸_____ 6:00.

Yuya: How ⁹_____ dinner? The movie finishes at 6:30.

Kaira: Okay. Umm … but I don't have much money.

Yuya: Don't ¹⁰_____. We know a good cheap place.

▶ Now complete Yuya and Kaira's Friday plans.

Yuya	Kaira
● Meet his ( )	● Have a ( )
● See a ( )	● Meet Yuya and his brother for ( )

❷ Using the expressions you have learned so far, fill in the blanks and practice these three mini-conversations with your partner.

1. **A:** The _____ is almost here.
   B: Yay! I'm really happy.
2. **A:** Do you want to _____ _____ karaoke after school?
   B: Of course! What time?
3. **A:** I have an English _____ _____ four o'clock.
   B: Let's meet after that!

Conversation B Sophie and Yuya are talking about how they spent the weekend.

❶ Listen to their conversation and complete the two key sentences.

Conversation 🎧 DL 10　◉ CD1-10　Key Sentences 🎧 DL 11　◉ CD1-11

Sophie: How was your weekend?

Yuya: I stayed home, but it was great. 💡1 **I was exhausted on** _____

_____ (7).　On Sunday, I cleaned my

apartment, put together a bookcase I had ordered, and watched my

favorite YouTube channel.　I feel recharged now.

Sophie: What an ideal weekend!　I love staying home too.　But last weekend,

I went camping with my cousin and some of his colleagues.

Yuya: Oh.　Does your cousin work in Japan?

Sophie: Yes, for a US-based company.

💡2 **He's really** _____

_____ (10).

He wants to sightsee while he's here, so

I've been visiting many places with him.

Yuya: Well, that sounds like fun.　But did you

forget?　There's a test tomorrow.

Sophie: Oh no!　I completely forgot!　I'll study

hard tonight.

❷ Take turns being A and B and practice this conversation with your partner.　You
can choose expressions from the hints or think of your own.

A: How was your weekend?

B: It was 　a　 .　I 　b　 and 　b　 on Saturday.　On Sunday I 　b　 .　What
did you do?

A: I 　b　 and 　b　 last weekend.

B: Well, that sounds 　c　 .

Hints
🔆

　a　 fantastic / fine / okay / terrible

　b　 ate out / saw a musical / visited relatives /
　　 played tennis / studied hard

　c　 like you had fun / busy / exciting

Expressing Yourself

Your Opinion Express your own view by answering the following question. Review the key sentences you learned on the previous page, if you like.

❓ Question

> Imagine two weekends: one where you stayed home and the other where you went out. What did you do?

—I was exhausted, so I _____

—I was busy last week, but I _____

Writing an Email Imagine that you had a wonderful weekend. What did you do? Fill out the chart and write an email to your high school friend.

▶ First, fill out the chart.

● Friday Evening	● Saturday	● Sunday
	Morning:	*Morning*:
	Afternoon:	*Afternoon*:
	Evening:	*Evening*:

▶ Next, complete the email with your own information.

○○○

Dear _____,

How are you? I was very busy last weekend.
First, I _____ . It was _____ .
Then, I _____ .
Finally, I _____ .
I was very tired on Sunday night, but I was happy.
How was your weekend? What did you do?

Love,

_____

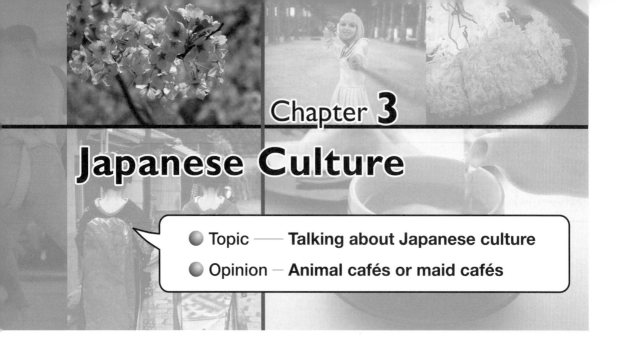

Chapter 3
Japanese Culture

- Topic —— **Talking about Japanese culture**
- Opinion — **Animal cafés or maid cafés**

Breaking the Ice

Fill in the blanks with your information, and then practice asking and answering the questions with your partner.   DL 12   CD1-12

1. Which of these words is also used in English: *jishin*, *tsunami*, or *arashi*?
   —I think _____ is used in English.
2. Which do you think is more popular with Japanese people, sumo or karate?
   —I think _____ is more popular.
3. Which do you think are more interesting, manga cafés or animal cafés?
   —I think _____ are more interesting.
4. Are you more interested in traditional Japanese culture or modern Japanese culture?
   —I'm more interested in _____ .

Getting the Topic

Vocabulary Matching Match each word or expression with its meaning.

1. loanword · · **a.** the way something is said
2. martial arts · · **b.** to take as one's own
3. be proud to · · **c.** to feel good about doing something
4. pronunciation · · **d.** a word that was originally from another language
5. adopt · · **e.** sports that involve fighting

Reading | Read the passage for information.

Japanese words in English

There are many Japanese loanwords in English. *Tycoon* (大君, great lord), for example, has been used for over a hundred years. In English, it means a rich business leader. The word *skosh* comes from 少し (a little). It was brought back to America by soldiers after WWII. Some older  Americans may not realize they are using a Japanese word when they say, "I'll have a skosh more coffee please." Other Japanese loanwords, such as 10 *sushi*, *geisha*, Kabuki, and Shinto are related to Japanese food, culture, and religion. Japanese martial arts have also contributed to English vocabulary by introducing *karate*, *judo*, and *dojo*.

Recently, young people worldwide have become very interested in Japanese pop culture. Some teenagers are proud to call themselves *otaku* because 15 they love Japanese *manga* and watch *anime*. One interesting fact about loanwords is when they are adopted into a new language, the pronunciation and the meaning often change. For example, the word *hibachi* (火鉢) is often pronounced "habachi" in the U.S., and it is a small barbecue grill for cooking meat. Through vocabulary, Japanese culture has spread throughout the 20 world.

5

True or False | Answer if the statement is true or false.

1. Some Japanese loanwords in English are over a hundred years old. [T / F]
2. In English, *skosh* means coffee. [T / F]
3. Japanese pop culture brought new words into English. [T / F]
4. Sometimes the pronunciation of Japanese words changes when they become English. [T / F]

Speaking Up

Conversation A Jack and Sophie are chatting about part-time jobs.

❶ Listen to their conversation and fill in the blanks. Next, practice it with your partner. 🎧 DL 14 💿 CD1-14

Jack: I'm applying for a job at a ¹_____ store.

Sophie: Don't you think it would be ²_____ to work at a Japanese restaurant?

Jack: Why? The ³_____ is about the same.

Sophie: You want to work ⁴_____ a hotel someday, right? You can learn how to talk to ⁵_____ politely if you work in a restaurant.

Jack: That's a pretty good idea.

Sophie: And don't forget, you can eat a lot of ⁶_____ food!

Jack: True! Maybe I'll ⁷_____ for a job at the *tonkatsu* restaurant next to the station instead! *Tonkatsu* is my ⁸_____! What are you going to do?

Sophie: I'm going to work ⁹_____ an intern at a translation company. I want to ¹⁰_____ my written Japanese.

▶ Now complete what Jack and Sophie will probably do.

```
Jack
● Apply for job at the
  (                    )
```

```
Sophie
● Work at a (            )
● Improve her (          )
```

❷ Using the expressions you have learned so far, fill in the blanks and practice these three mini-conversations with your partner.

1. A: I'm _____ for a job at a hotel.
   B: Don't you think it _____ be _____ to work at a *ryokan*?

2. A: You can learn about Japanese culture working in a *ryokan*.
   B: That's a pretty _____ _____!

3. A: What are you _____ to do?
   B: I'm going to _____ as an _____ at a trading company.

Conversation B The international club members are deciding what to do on the weekend.

❶ Listen to their conversation and complete the two key sentences.

Conversation 🎧 DL 15 ◉ CD1-15   **Key Sentences** 🎧 DL 16 ◉ CD1-16

Mai: Let's visit a themed café this weekend.
Yuya: Great idea. 💡1 _____ (4).
          They _____ (4).
Angelo: Animals? How about something more
          exciting, like a café with robot waiters
          or a vampire decor?
Kaira: Actually, I'm interested in *otaku*
          culture, so I'd like to go to a maid café.
Angelo: What's a maid café?
Kaira: 💡2 **The waitresses** _____
          _____ (10). They say it is a typical form of *omotenashi*.
Mai: Doesn't that sound like fun, Yuya? We can play silly games and have
          fun conversations with the maids!
Yuya: Well, I don't know…
Angelo: Oh, come on, Yuya. It sounds fun! Let's go to one!

❷ Take turns being A, B, and C and practice this conversation with two friends.
   You can choose expressions from the hints or think of your own.

A: What shall we do this weekend?
B: It's a good day to go to   a .
A: Maybe. But how about something different?   b   are fun. I went to one
    c .
C: Sounds fun, but let's do something cheaper. There's   d   I want to go to.
B: Oh, yeah. I'm broke.
A: All right. Let's go there!

Hints

a	an aquarium / a craft beer bar / a skating rink
b	bird cafés / bowling alleys / city pools
c	last month / about a year ago / just yesterday
d	a free exhibition / a public lecture / a park

Expressing Yourself

Your Opinion Express your own view by answering the following question. Review the key sentences you learned on the previous page, if you like.

❓ Question

> A foreign friend of yours wants to go to a themed café in Japan. Which do you recommend, an animal café or a maid café?

—I recommend an animal café because _____

—I think a maid café is better. That's because _____

_____

Writing a Review Imagine you are writing a review of a tourist attraction for the International Student Newspaper.

▶ First, circle the place you want to review and then fill in the information.

● Tourist attractions
  Ryogoku Sumo Hall / Nara Park / Okinawa Churaumi Aquarium /
  Goryokaku Tower / Kusatsu Onsen Resort / Other _____
● Basic information
  Location _____
  Admission fee _____
  Highlight _____

▶ Now complete the article about a place you recommend for international students.

A Must-see in Japan!

_____ is the place international students should visit.

It is located in _____ .

It { is / isn't } expensive. The cost is ¥ _____ .

I recommend this place because _____ .

22

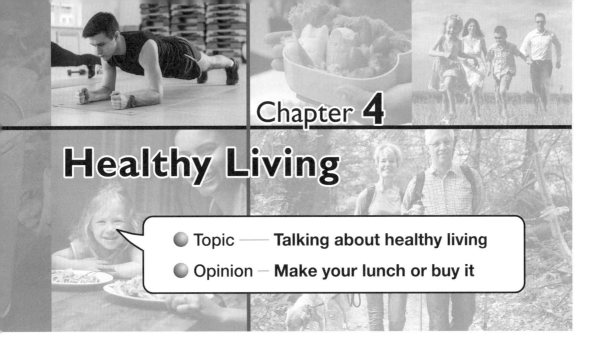

Chapter 4

Healthy Living

- Topic —— **Talking about healthy living**
- Opinion — **Make your lunch or buy it**

Breaking the Ice

Fill in the blanks with your information, and then practice asking and answering the questions with your partner.　　　　　　　　　　　　　DL 17　　CD1-17

1. How many minutes do you walk every day?
   —I walk for about _____ a day.
2. Did you eat a heavy or light meal last night?
   —I ate _____.
3. Who is the oldest person you know?
   —The oldest person I know is _____.
4. Do you feel tired or refreshed when you get up in the morning?
   —I feel _____ when I get up.

Getting the Topic

Vocabulary Matching Match each word or expression with its meaning.

1. gain access to	·	· **a.**	to stop a disease or sickness
2. nutritious	·	· **b.**	a treatment to prevent catching a disease
3. life expectancy	·	· **c.**	how long a person will probably live
4. cure	·	· **d.**	to be able to get something
5. vaccination	·	· **e.**	something that is healthy and good for you

Living a long and healthy life

"Human life expectancy" refers to the average length of time a person is expected to live. It varies from country to country because of differences in economic circumstances, medical care, and daily diet. Life expectancy differs for men and women because women tend to live longer than men. Today, the worldwide average life expectancy is 71 years, but a little over a hundred years ago, it was around 40. One reason for this increase is fewer children are dying. In the 20th century, scientists invented vaccinations to prevent childhood diseases and medicines to cure them. Additionally, people gained access to more nutritious food.

5

10

Japan has the longest life expectancy in the world now. Perhaps the biggest reason for this is the Japanese diet, which consists of various fresh fruits and vegetables. Portion sizes are small and food is often grilled or steamed. Additionally, many people use public transportation to go to work, so they often walk or bicycle to the station. Some companies even have morning exercises for their workers. Japan's life expectancy continues to increase. Can you imagine living until the 22nd century?

15

20

True or False Answer if the statement is true or false.

1. Human life expectancy is the same for men and women. [T / F]

2. Today the average global life expectancy is over 70. [T / F]

3. People live longer today because doctors found cures for many diseases. [T / F]

4. Japanese people eat large portions and rarely exercise. [T / F]

Speaking Up

Conversation A Jack and Mai are studying at a fast food restaurant after school.

❶ Listen to their conversation and fill in the blanks. Next, practice it with your partner.

Mai: Isn't it too early to have dinner?

Jack: This isn't dinner! It's my ¹_____.

Mai: Your snack is two hamburgers, an extra-large order of ²_____, and a chocolate milkshake?

Jack: Well, I'm starving! I ³_____ ⁴_____ at the gym earlier.

Mai: I know you're hungry, but you ⁵_____ eat ⁶_____ food.

Jack: I know, but fast food is cheap and ⁷_____.

Mai: My favorite restaurant is near the school. It's a buffet and not very ⁸_____. There are many healthy choices.

Jack: Where is it?

Mai: It's ten minutes by bus or thirty minutes on ⁹_____. I usually walk so I can combine exercise ¹⁰_____ healthy eating.

Jack: Sounds great! Let's go tomorrow.

▶ Now complete the following information about Jack and Mai.

Jack's order	Mai's favorite restaurant
• Two ( )	= A ( ) restaurant
• Extra-large ( )	• Has many ( )
• A chocolate ( )	• ( ) by bus

❷ Using the expressions you have learned so far, fill in the blanks and practice these three mini-conversations with your partner.

1. **A:** Your snack is three rice balls, instant noodles, and a large cola?
   B: Well, I'm _____! I worked out at the gym in the afternoon.
2. **A:** You _____ eat healthier food.
   B: I know, but fast food is _____ and _____.
3. **A:** There's a good vegetarian restaurant near here. It's not _____.
   B: Sounds great! Let's _____ tomorrow.

Conversation B Angelo, Mai, Kaira, and Jack are talking about how to have a long and healthy life.

❶ Listen to their conversation and complete the two key sentences.

Conversation 🎧 DL 20 ◉CD1-20 **Key Sentences** 🎧 DL 21 ◉CD1-21

Angelo: I called my grandmother today. It's her 90th birthday.

Mai: She's 90! What's her secret to a long life?

Angelo: She said the most important thing is to laugh a lot. She also cooks healthy food every day.

Kaira: 🔑1 **That's great advice, but** _____

_____ (10) **than to make it.**

Mai: Not necessarily. You have to plan well.

Kaira: Yeah, but how?

Mai: I go shopping just once a week. I cook a lot on Sundays. I make a variety of dishes to eat for the entire week. I put them in small containers and freeze them.

Jack: 🔑2 **Thanks to Mai's advice, I started** _____ (3).

_____ (4) **a day**!

Mai: But you still eat fried food almost every night at your restaurant.

❷ Take turns being A and B and practice this conversation with your partner. You can choose expressions from the hints or think of your own.

A: What's your secret to a healthy life?

B: The most important thing is to a . I also b .

A: Those are great ideas.

B: How about you? Do you do anything to stay healthy?

A: Well, I eat healthy food like c and c .

Hints 💡

a	exercise a lot / get enough sleep / cook healthy food everyday
b	drink green tea / chat with friends to relieve stress / play with my dog
c	fresh fruit / *soba* / brown rice

Expressing Yourself

Your Opinion Express your own view by answering the following questions. Review the key sentences you learned on the previous page, if you like.

? Questions

> Do you make your lunch or buy it? Why or why not?

—I make my lunch every day. That way, I can _____

—I usually buy my lunch because _____

—It depends. I _____

Writing a Survey Write a survey to find out about students' healthy habits.

▶ First, check the items that you think are important.

☐ sleep eight hours every night　　☐ eat a healthy breakfast
☐ exercise every day　　　　　　　☐ don't smoke
☐ eat a lot of vegetables　　　　　☐ don't drink too much alcohol
☐ others _____ _____ _____

▶ Next, write the survey questions. The first question is done for you.

● Health Survey ●

1. How many hours do you sleep at night?
2. _____
3. _____
4. _____
5. _____
6. _____

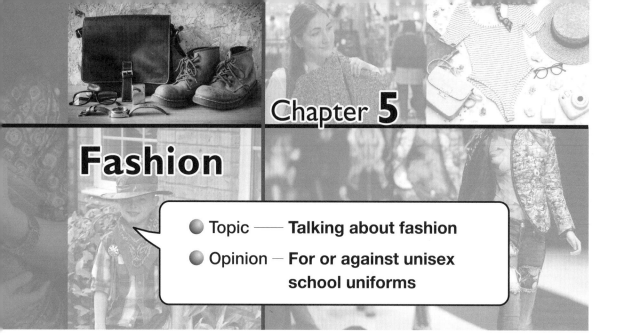

Chapter **5**

Fashion

- ● Topic —— **Talking about fashion**
- ● Opinion — **For or against unisex school uniforms**

Breaking the Ice

Fill in the blanks with your information, and then practice asking and answering the questions with your partner. 🎧 DL 22 💿 CD1-22

1. Do you shop online or go to a store to buy new clothes?
　　—I usually _____ to buy new clothes.
2. What clothes did you last buy?
　　—I bought _____.
3. Which do you like better, trendy or classic styles?
　　—I like _____ better.
4. Which do you prefer having, a lot of clothes that are inexpensive or fewer clothes that are expensive?
　　—I prefer having _____.

Getting the Topic

Vocabulary Matching) Match each word or expression with its meaning.

1. products　　　·
2. competition　·
3. accuse　　　·
4. veil　　　　·
5. controversial ·

· **a.** to claim someone did something wrong
· **b.** causing disagreement or discussion
· **c.** things that are bought and sold
· **d.** the activity of trying to win
· **e.** covering for the face or head

Read the passage for information.

A controversial fashion ad

DL 23　　CD1-23

Most young people like to look fashionable. When they go shopping, they have a wide range of fashion brands to choose from. These brands fit their lifestyles, personalities, and budgets. Because so many items are available, the competition for customers is severe. To attract new customers, companies advertise their products through traditional advertising methods as well as social media, which includes Instagram, Facebook, and YouTube.

Recently, a clothing company released an advertisement on social media that was very controversial. In this video, an Israeli woman was wearing a veil and headscarf often worn by Muslim women. Only her eyes were showing. The woman removed the veil and headscarf to show jeans and a T-shirt. She was a famous supermodel. She shook her hair and began to dance to music promoting the company's "Freedom is Basic" campaign. This ad caused immediate outrage on social media and the company was accused of racism and hatred. One blogger wrote that the ad disrespected an entire country, an entire gender, and an entire religion to sell a T-shirt. What do you think of this controversy? How far should companies go to sell products?

True or False Answer if the statement is true or false.

1. Many young people select clothes and accessories to show their personality.

[T / F]

2. A supermodel was in an advertising campaign to sell headscarves.　[T / F]

3. No one complained about the "Freedom is Basic" campaign.　　　[T / F]

4. One blogger believed the ad showed respect for other cultures.　　[T / F]

Speaking Up

Conversation A Kaira is telling Mai about an uncomfortable experience she had recently.

❶ Listen to their conversation and fill in the blanks. Next, practice it with your partner. 🎧 DL 24   💿 CD1-24

Kaira: I'm pretty ¹_____ today.

Mai: Why? What ²_____?

Kaira: I was invited to a community center to talk about India. The lady in charge ³_____ me to wear a sari to show Indian culture.

Mai: Well, your saris *are* beautiful.

Kaira: I know. But she ⁴_____ ⁵_____ the group my sari was a costume! She made me feel ⁶_____ I had dressed up for Halloween.

Mai: That's terrible!

Kaira: I wanted to ask her if she thought Japanese kimonos were costumes, too.

Mai: I guess it's easy to think of clothes from other countries ⁷_____ ⁸_____. What seems normal to us seems exotic to ⁹_____.

Kaira: I suppose ¹⁰_____ right. I went to a party in India. A Korean girl wore a beautiful *hanbok*. Everyone wanted to ask her about it.

▶ Now complete the following information.

```
What happened to Kaira
● Invited to the (                    ) to talk about (            )
● Wore a (              )
● The lady called Kaira's sari a (                ) → Kaira was (            )
```

❷ Using the expressions you have learned so far, fill in the blanks and then practice these three mini-conversations with your partner.

1. **A:** My friend was pretty _____ today.
   B: Why? _____ happened?
2. **A:** My mother keeps telling me that I shouldn't color my hair.
   B: That's _____!
3. **A:** What seems normal to us sometimes seems rude to others.
   B: I _____ you're _____.

Conversation B Mai, Sophie, Yuya, and Jack are talking about school uniforms.

❶ Listen to their conversation and complete the two key sentences.

Conversation 🎧 DL 25 ⊙ CD1-25 Key Sentences 🎧 DL 26 ⊙ CD1-26

Mai: Look at those girls. I went to the same high school and wore that uniform.

Sophie: Wasn't it boring to wear the same clothes every day?

Mai: Not really. I never had to decide what to wear.

Yuya: Mai's right. It was very easy to get dressed every morning.

Jack: Uniforms are easy. In Australia, we wear high school uniforms too. But the rules in Japan seem much stricter.

Mai: It depends on the school. Some schools are very strict.

Sophie: 🎧₁ **I read in the newspaper** _____

_____ (9).

Mai: That's great news. 🎧₂ **We** _____

_____ (7). It would have been warmer to wear pants.

❷ Take turns being A and B and practice this conversation with your partner. You can choose expressions from the hints or think of your own.

A: What did you think about your school uniform?

B: I { liked / didn't like } it. It was ▢ a ▢ because I ▢ b ▢.

A: Were the rules strict at your school?

B: ▢ c ▢. We { were / weren't } allowed to ▢ d ▢.

Hints

a	boring / great / convenient
b	had to wear the same thing every day / liked the design / didn't have to choose what to wear
c	Not really / They really were / So-so
d	dye our hair / have pierced ears / modify our uniforms at all

Expressing Yourself

Your Opinion Express your own view by answering the following question. Review the key sentences you learned on the previous page, if you like.

❓ Question

What do you think of the move to have unisex school uniforms?

—I agree with the idea. In high school, _____

—I'm against the idea because _____

—I'm not sure, but _____

Writing a Review Imagine you had 10,000 yen and you ordered something to wear from an online shop. Write an online review for what you bought.

▶ First, fill in the following information.

- ● How many stars _____ (one to five: 5=excellent/1=poor)
- ● What you bought _____ (T-shirt, pants, sneakers, etc.)
- ● Why you bought it / them _____ (school, a party, a club event, etc.)
- ● Fit _____ (too large, too small, perfect, etc.)
- ● Color _____
- ● Price _____

▶ Next, complete your online review.

○○○

☆☆☆☆☆
I recently bought { a / an / some } _____.
I bought { it / them } to wear to _____.
The size was _____ for me.
The color { looks good / doesn't look good } on me.
The price was _____, { so / but } I { would / wouldn't }
buy { it / them } again.

32

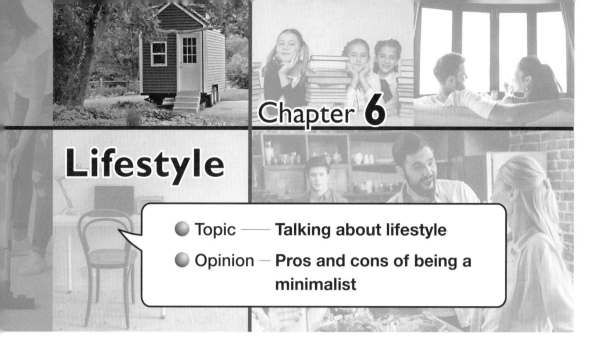

Chapter 6

Lifestyle

- ● Topic —— **Talking about lifestyle**
- ● Opinion — **Pros and cons of being a minimalist**

Breaking the Ice

Fill in the blanks with your information, and then practice asking and answering the questions with your partner.
 DL 27 CD1-27

1. What do you do with clothes, books, or other things you don't want any more? Do you throw them away or keep them?
   —I _____.

2. Is your desk cluttered or is it tidy?
   —It's _____.

3. Do you want to live in various cities or stay in one city?
   —I want to _____.

4. Have you ever bought anything that you wished later you hadn't? If so, what was it?
   —No, _____. / Yes, I bought _____.

Getting the Topic

Vocabulary Matching Match each word or expression with its meaning.

1. minimal   ·   · **a.** to put things where they belong
2. lifestyle   ·   · **b.** having an impact
3. clutter   ·   · **c.** the least amount
4. tidy up   ·   · **d.** the way people live
5. influential ·   · **e.** to make a mess with things everywhere

Living with less: Minimalism

DL 28 CD1-28

Some people nowadays like to own fewer things. These people, who are called minimalists, say they do not need many things to be happy. Instead, they only buy things they truly need. What are the benefits of a minimalist lifestyle? First, our homes will be neater. Too many things make our homes cluttered. We can also save a lot of time because we have fewer things to clean and take care of. We can also work less because we won't have to worry about earning enough money to spend on things that we don't really need.

Several years ago, a Japanese woman named Marie Kondo wrote a book on how to organize your life to live with fewer things. She loved tidying up as a child and even wrote her college graduation thesis on this topic. Her book became a bestseller in the United States after it was translated into English. Many people started following the "KonMari Method." They decluttered their homes and kept only the things that made them happy. She became so popular that *Time* magazine listed her as one of the most influential people in 2015, and in 2019, she became a television star.

5

10

15

20

True or False Answer if the statement is true or false.

1. People who like to own many things are called minimalists. [T / F]

2. Minimalists say having fewer things will help us save time. [T / F]

3. Marie Kondo didn't like straightening up as a child. [T / F]

4. Marie Kondo believes that people should own things that make them unhappy as well as happy. [T / F]

Speaking Up

Conversation A Sophie is giving advice to Jack on how to tidy up his room before his mother visits.

❶ Listen to their conversation and fill in the blanks. Then practice it with your partner. 🎧 DL 29 ⦿ CD1-29

Jack: My mother is ¹_____ from Australia to visit me.

Sophie: That sounds fun.

Jack: Yeah, but I don't ²_____ ³_____ to see my messy room. There are books, ⁴_____, and papers everywhere. And there's a lot of garbage too. Ahh ....

Sophie: I'll tell you ⁵_____ to solve your problem. I love to ⁶_____ things.

Jack: That'd be great!

Sophie: First, divide everything ⁷_____ three piles. One is for ⁸_____. Another is for things to keep. The third is for things to sell.

Jack: To sell?

Sophie: Yes. There's a resale shop near the station. You can sell large items like sports ⁹_____ there.

Jack: Can you come over and help me clean?

Sophie: Nope. You made the mess. You have to ¹⁰_____ it up. But I'll help you take things to the resale shop.

▶ Now complete Sophie's advice for cleaning Jack's room.

Divide everything into (   )
- One for (   )
- Another for (   )
- The third for (   )

❷ Using the expressions you have learned so far, fill in the blanks and then practice these three mini-conversations with your partner.

1. **A:** My brother is coming from Okinawa to _____ me.
   B: That _____ great!

2. **A:** I don't know how to tidy up my _____ room ....
   B: OK. I'll tell you how to _____ your problem.

3. **A:** Can you come _____ and _____ me clean?
   B: No way. You have to do it yourself.

❶ Listen to their conversation and complete the two key sentences.

Conversation 🎧 DL 30 ⦿CD1-30 Key Sentences 🎧 DL 31 ⦿CD1-31

Jack: Look at this YouTube video. This couple lives in a tiny house on wheels! I want to have a simple life like they do. Wouldn't it be great?

Kaira: Not for me. 🔑1 _____

_____ (8).

Jack: But they have a lot of freedom.

🔑2 **They can easily** _____

_____ (9) **with them**.

Kaira: But there's no place to put things like comics! I can't live without my Japanese *manga*.

Jack: I read everything on my phone, so I'm okay with that.

Kaira: And you can't invite people over. You'd only have dishes and seats for two.

Jack: But don't you think it would be fun to live like that for a while?

Kaira: Maybe. If you're with someone you really like.

Jack: I totally agree.

❷ Take turns being A and B and practice this conversation with your partner. You can choose expressions from the hints or think of your own.

A: I'm going to get rid of a lot of my ▢ a ▢. I want to have a simpler life.

B: That's not for me. I like having ▢ b ▢.

A: Owning fewer things means we can ▢ c ▢.

B: Well, good luck! Enjoy your new lifestyle. By the way, if you are going to throw away your ▢ d ▢, can I have { it / them }?

Hints

▢ a ▢	DVDs / comic books / clothes
▢ b ▢	a lot of CDs / tons of clothes / lots of cute dishes
▢ c ▢	save time with less to clean / have a neater place / appreciate what we have
▢ d ▢	handbags / soccer magazines / card collection

Expressing Yourself

Your Opinion Express your own view by answering the following questions. Review the key sentences you learned on the previous page, if you like.

❓ Questions

> Do you want to try living as a minimalist? Why or why not?

—I want to be a minimalist because _____

—It would be fun to be one for a while, but _____

—I don't want to be a minimalist at all. I _____

Writing an Email Imagine you have moved to a tiny apartment and need to get rid of many things. Ask a friend if he/she wants some of the things you don't need.

▶ First, check five things you no longer need.

☐ stove ☐ fridge ☐ frying pan ☐ coffee maker ☐ high school textbooks
☐ computer ☐ comic books ☐ dolls ☐ soccer ball ☐ baseball uniform
☐ guitar ☐ speakers ☐ other _____

▶ Next, write an email to your friend asking if he or she wants to have any of the things you don't want.

Hi _____ ,

Today I moved to a tiny apartment. It is so small! I want to give away some things. Would you like to have my _____ ,

_____ , or _____ ?

I also want to give away my _____ and _____ .

I think you'll like the _____ because _____

_____ .

If you'd like any of these things, please let me know by _____ .
I'll help you carry them to your place.

Best,

_____

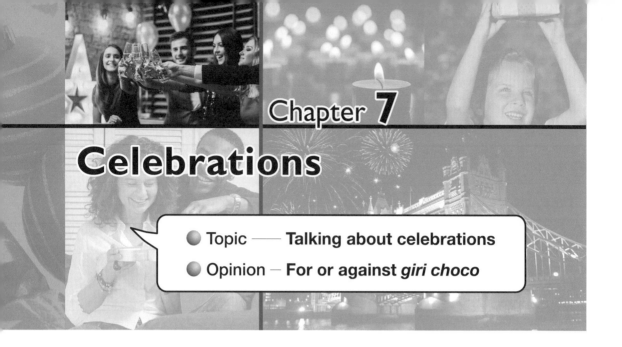

Chapter **7**

Celebrations

- Topic —— **Talking about celebrations**
- Opinion — **For or against *giri choco***

Breaking the Ice

Fill in the blanks with your information, and then practice asking and answering the questions with your partner. 🎧 DL 32 💿 CD1-32

1. When is your birthday?

　—It's _____.

2. Which do you like better, parties at home or parties in restaurants?

　—I like _____ better.

3. What's your favorite celebration?

　—My favorite celebration is _____.

4. Do you prefer spending holidays with your friends or your family?

　—I prefer spending holidays _____.

Getting the Topic

Vocabulary Matching | Match each word or expression with its meaning.

1. copyright ·
2. earn ·
3. royalties ·
4. expire ·
5. judge ·

· **a.** the person who makes decisions in a court
· **b.** a percentage of money paid, based on sales
· **c.** to make money
· **d.** exclusive and legal ownership
· **e.** to become no longer valid

Read the passage for information.

The highest earning song

DL 33   CD1-33

Do you know what song has made more money than any other song? It's a song that everyone knows and that everyone can sing. It's the "Happy Birthday" song.

5

The words were written by two American sisters in 1893. It wasn't until 1935 that the song was copyrighted. Whenever the "Happy Birthday" song was played in public, royalties had to be paid to the copyright owners.

10

Warner Brothers, a large entertainment company, bought the company that owned the copyright in 1988 for $25 million. When people sang "Happy Birthday" in movies or TV shows, producers had to pay Warner Brothers a lot of money. For example, Disney had to pay $5,000 just to use the song in a parade.

15

The company earned $2 million dollars a year from the "Happy Birthday" song. Many people said the song belongs to everyone because the copyright expired a long time ago. A judge agreed and decided that the company had to return money to people who had paid to use the song. From now on, people can sing "Happy Birthday" anywhere they like without having to pay.

20

True or False Answer if the statement is true or false.

1. Everybody knows the "Happy Birthday" song, but it is a mystery who wrote it. [T / F]
2. The Happy Birthday song was copyrighted in 1893. [T / F]
3. Warner Brothers earned $5,000 dollars a year from this song. [T / F]
4. A judge agreed that the company could continue charging people for using this song. [T / F]

Speaking Up

Conversation A Yuya is calling a restaurant to make a reservation.

❶ Listen to their conversation and fill in the blanks. Then practice it with your partner.   🎧 DL 34   💿 CD1-34

Yuya: Hello, I'd like to make a ¹_____ for Friday night.
Restaurant: Sure! ²_____ how many people? And ³_____ time?
Yuya: There'll be six ⁴_____ us. Would 7:00 be okay?
Restaurant: Sorry, but there are no tables ⁵_____ until 7:30.
Yuya: Oh, okay. I guess that's ⁶_____ . It's a birthday party.
                Can you keep ⁷_____ for us until dessert?
Restaurant: No problem.
Yuya: And is it ⁸_____ to play the Beatles during dinner?
                That's the birthday girl's favorite music.
Restaurant: I'm sorry, but we can't do that. However, we can prepare a
                ⁹_____ dessert and the ¹⁰_____ can sing "Happy
                Birthday."
Yuya: That sounds nice. She'll be happy. Oh, and her name is Sophie.

▶ Now complete Yuya's requests and the restaurant's response.

Yuya's requests	Responses
● Keep (	) → OK / No
● Play (	) → OK / No, but can prepare a ( )

❷ Using the expressions you have learned so far, fill in the blanks and then practice these three mini-conversations with your partner.

1. A: I'd like to make a _____ for Friday night.
   B: Sure! For _____ _____ people?
2. A: _____ 7:00 be okay?
   B: Sorry, but _____ _____ no tables available until 8:00.
3. A: Can you _____ the Beatles _____ dinner?
   B: No, but we can _____ a special dessert and sing "_____
          _____."

40

Conversation B Mai is telling Sophie about Valentine's Day in Japan.

❶ Listen to their conversation and complete the two key sentences.

Conversation 🎧 DL 35   ◉ CD1-35   **Key Sentences** 🎧 DL 36   ◉ CD1-36

Mai: Valentine's Day in Japan started in the 1950s. It was advertised as the day a woman could tell a man she liked him by buying him chocolates.

Sophie: But didn't women start buying chocolates for all the men they knew?

Mai: Yes. That's called *giri choco*. Obligation chocolate.

Sophie: 🔑1 **I heard that** _____
_____ (10).

Mai: Yeah, my sister works at a company. She says it's too expensive to buy chocolates for everyone.

Sophie: I guess the confectionary companies will lose money if the custom stops.

Mai: Maybe not. Nowadays there's *honmei choco*, *tomo choco*, and *jibun choco*.

Sophie: Huh? Oh! I get it! Chocolate for the person you really love, chocolate for your friends, and chocolate for yourself.

Mai: That's right. 🔑2 **Personally, I think** _____
_____ (11).

❷ Take turns being A and B and practice this conversation with your partner. You can choose expressions from the hints or think of your own.

A: What do you think of { giving / getting } Valentine's Day chocolates?
B: To be honest, I ▨ a ▨ chocolates { for / from } my friends.
A: Really? Why?
B: It ▨ b ▨ . By the way, what do you think of *jibun choco*?
A: Buying chocolates for myself? I think it's a ▨ c ▨ idea. I'll ▨ d ▨ .

Hints
:💡:
- a   enjoy making / don't enjoy getting / love receiving
- b   gets expensive / takes a lot of time to make / makes my friends happy
- c   great / silly / strange
- d   never do that / buy some next year / see what's on sale

Expressing Yourself

Your Opinion Express your own view by answering the following questions. Review the key sentences you learned on the previous page, if you like.

? Questions

What do you think of the custom of *giri choco*? Do you think it's a good custom or do you want it to stop?

—I think *giri choco* is good because _____

—I'm not sure, but _____

—I don't like the custom. For one thing, _____

Writing an Invitation Imagine you are going to have a party. Think of the details about the party and then write the invitation.

▶ First, fill in the following information.

- Type of party _____ (surprise, Christmas, welcome, etc.)
- Place _____ (restaurant, home, bar, etc.)
- Date and time _____
- Dress code _____
- Cost _____
- What to bring _____

▶ Next, complete your invitation.

🍷 Party Time!

You are invited to a _____ party.

It will be held on _____ at _____ .

It is going to be { casual / formal } so please wear _____ clothes.

The cost per person is _____ . Please bring _____ .

Looking forward to seeing you there!

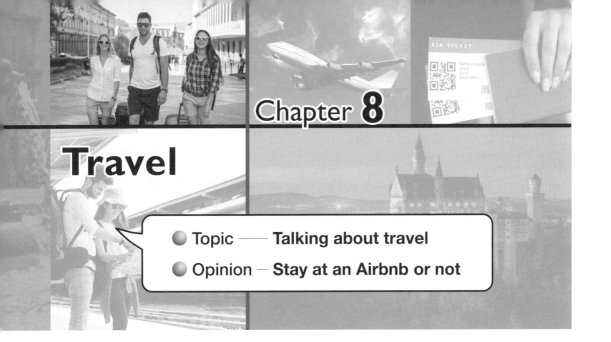

Chapter 8

Travel

- Topic —— **Talking about travel**
- Opinion — **Stay at an Airbnb or not**

Breaking the Ice

Fill in the blanks with your information, and then practice asking and answering the questions with your partner.

DL 37   CD1-37

1. How often do you take a trip? About once a year or more often?
   —I take a trip _____.
2. Do you prefer traveling alone, with family, or with friends?
   —I prefer traveling _____.
3. Which do you like better, visiting historical sites or seeing beautiful nature?
   —I like _____ better.
4. Which do you prefer, going on short trips or long trips?
   —I prefer going on _____.

Getting the Topic

Vocabulary Matching Match each word or expression with its meaning.

1. experience   ·   · **a.** usual
2. accommodation ·   · **b.** to travel to new places
3. comfortable   ·   · **c.** to take part in or to do
4. explore   ·   · **d.** a place to stay
5. ordinary   ·   · **e.** making you feel relaxed

Alternative places to stay

DL 38   CD1-38

In 1909, a German elementary school teacher came up with the idea of cheap hotels for young people. He believed that they should be allowed to travel and experience different cultures cheaply and safely. The first youth

©Shonenji Temple Lodge

5

hostel was opened in a beautiful castle in Germany in 1912. Since then, 10
youth hostels have opened all over the world and now there are more than
4,000 youth hostels in 87 countries.

In recent years, Airbnb rentals have become popular. Airbnb is a company
with an online marketplace where people rent out their rooms or homes to
travelers. This system began in 2008, and now millions of people have 15
stayed at Airbnb properties. Tourists can choose from many kinds of
accommodation. For example, there is a 450-year-old temple in Takachiho,
Kyushu that accepts Airbnb guests in its lodging. Japanese and
international visitors can enjoy comfortable accommodations while exploring
the temple grounds and local area. 20

The advantages of staying in a youth hostel or an Airbnb are meeting
people and having experiences you couldn't have in an ordinary hotel. How
about staying at one for your next trip?

True or False Answer if the statement is true or false.

1. A German doctor thought hotels for young people should be cheap. [T / F]
2. There are more than 5,000 youth hostels in 87 countries. [T / F]
3. People can rent out their rooms or homes through Airbnb. [T / F]
4. A 450-year-old temple is an Airbnb property. [T / F]

Speaking Up

Conversation A Kaira and Mai are talking about sightseeing spots in Tokyo.

❶ Listen to their conversation and fill in the blanks. Next, practice it with your partner. 🎧 DL 39 💿 CD1-39

Kaira: My aunt will be visiting Tokyo on a business trip. She has one free day and I'm going to ¹_____ her ²_____.

Mai: Only one day? That's too short.

Kaira: I know! Do you have any ³_____?

Mai: Why ⁴_____ you show her historical places in the morning and ⁵_____ places in the afternoon?

Kaira: What do you mean?

Mai: You could visit Meiji Shrine first. Then go to Asakusa. The ⁶_____ and the ⁷_____ shops are very popular with tourists.

Kaira: Hmm. We could have ⁸_____ there and then go to Akihabara. After that I'll ⁹_____ her to Ginza.

Mai: I'm sure you'll plan a day she'll never ¹⁰_____.

▶ Now complete where Kaira will probably take her aunt.

```
Showing around Tokyo
● visit (                    ) first
● go to (              ) → the temple and (                    )
● eat lunch in (              ) and go to (            ) and
  (            )
```

❷ Using the expressions you have learned so far, fill in the blanks and then practice these three mini-conversations with your partner.

1. A: I want to show my cousin _____ Kyoto, but he has just one free day.

   B: Only one day? That's _____ _____!

2. A: _____ don't you show him both historical and modern places?

   B: What do you _____?

3. A: We could have tofu cuisine at Nanzenji Temple and then go to Kyoto Tower.

   B: I'm sure you'll _____ a day we'll _____ forget!

Conversation B Kaira, Yuya, Mai, and Jack are talking about their summer vacation plans.

❶ Listen to their conversation and complete the two key sentences.

Conversation 🎧 DL 40 ◎ CD1-40 **Key Sentences** 🎧 DL 41 ◎ CD1-41

Kaira: I can't wait for our summer vacation. I really want to experience more of Japan.

Yuya: Miyazaki Prefecture is an ideal place for that. There's a lot to see and the food is great.

Mai: 🔑1 **I found a good Airbnb for us.** _____

_____ (7).

Yuya: An Airbnb? The other day I read that there have been some problems with them.

🔑2 **Sometimes** _____

_____ (8).

Jack: I also heard that sometimes guests and hosts can't communicate with each other.

Mai: I don't think we'll have that problem. You guys can speak Japanese to our hosts.

Yuya: We'll still have to be careful about noise.

Mai: True. We'll be staying in a 450-year-old temple in Takachiho. There won't be any neighbors to disturb, but we'll have to be respectful of the surroundings!

❷ Take turns being A and B and practice this conversation with your partner. You can choose expressions from the hints or think of your own.

A: I can't wait for   a ! I'm planning to visit   b .

B: How exciting! What do you want to do there?

A: I want to   c .

B: b   seems like an ideal place for that. You can also   d   there.

Hints
- 💡
  - a   Golden Week / summer vacation / the New Year's holidays
  - b   the Tohoku Region / Italy / Australia
  - c   visit hot springs / try the food there / relax at a beach
  - d   see old and modern architecture / stay at a beachside cottage / go camping

46

Expressing Yourself

Your Opinion Express your own view by answering the following questions. Review the key sentences you learned on the previous page, if you like.

? **Questions**

> Do you want to stay at an Airbnb if you have a chance? If so, what is the advantage of an Airbnb? If not, what is a possible problem with an Airbnb?

—I { want to stay / have stayed } at an Airbnb. I think one advantage of

Airbnb is that _____

—I don't want to stay at an Airbnb. I think one problem is that _____

_____

Writing an Ad Imagine you are going to open a hostel in your hometown. You need an English website for international guests.

▶ First, think of what kind of hostel it is going to be.

- Hostel name _____
- Location _____
- Nearest station _____
- Atmosphere _____ (casual, friendly, lively, etc.)
- Facilities _____ (a kitchen, pool, tennis court, etc.)
- Breakfast _____ (western-style, Japanese-style, none)
- Other features _____ (bicycle rentals, barbecue area)

▶ Next, complete the details for your website.

○○○

_____ is located in _____ , just _____ minutes away from _____ station. We can offer you a _____ atmosphere at a reasonable price.

We have _____ and _____ .

Breakfast is _____ .

We also have _____ .

Chapter 9

Food

- Topic —— **Talking about food**
- Opinion — **The best Japanese food**

Breaking the Ice

Fill in the blanks with your information, and then practice asking and answering the questions with your partner. 　DL 42　　CD2-02

1. What is your favorite food?

　—My favorite food is _____.

2. What food do you dislike?

　—I dislike _____.

3. Which of these foods would you like to try:　Thai, Filipino, Mexican, or German?

　—I'd like to try _____ food.

4. Which do you prefer, western food or Japanese food?

　—I prefer _____.

Getting the Topic

Vocabulary Matching Match each word or expression with its meaning.

1. pioneer · · **a.** people from one country who live in another

2. expatriates · · **b.** can find anywhere

3. celebrities · · **c.** to change

4. widely available · · **d.** a person who is the first to do something

5. shift · · **e.** famous people

Japanese food in the world

Before the 1980s, there were few Japanese restaurants in foreign countries. JETRO says Japanese food became popular abroad in three stages. The first stage is called "pioneer days." This was when the restaurant customers shifted from Japanese expatriates to the local people. In California, Japanese food became popular because of Hollywood celebrities. Celebrities were among the first non-Japanese to eat sushi. 10 Tempura and sukiyaki were also popular.

The second stage is the "development period." Japanese food items, such as soy sauce and *mirin* became available in local supermarkets. In addition, Japanese fruit and vegetables began to be grown locally.

As Japanese food became more familiar to people, they wanted to eat the 15 same food that Japanese people eat. This stage is called the "realistic period" because a greater variety of Japanese dishes became widely available. Many restaurants serving ordinary Japanese food opened, and for the first time, people could eat *udon*, ramen, and curry in them.

Japanese food was at first considered strange and exotic, and Japanese 20 restaurants were too expensive for most people. Nowadays you can find them almost anywhere around the world.

True or False | Answer if the statement is true or false.

1. Before 1980, there were few Japanese restaurants throughout the United States.　　　　　　　　　　　　　　　　　　　　　　　　　[T / F]
2. Sushi was immediately popular with everyone.　　　　　　　　[T / F]
3. Eventually Japanese vegetables became available, but not Japanese seasonings.　　　　　　　　　　　　　　　　　　　　　　　　[T / F]
4. Japanese restaurants can now be found all over the world.　　　[T / F]

Speaking Up

Conversation A Kaira, Sophie, and Yuya surprise Jack by going to the *tonkatsu* restaurant he works at.

❶ Listen to their conversation and fill in the blanks. Next, practice it with your group.

🎧 DL 44 💿 CD2-04

Jack:	*Irasshaimase*! Oh! It's you ¹_____! What are you doing here?
Kaira:	We came to have dinner at your ²_____!
Jack:	This is a fantastic ³_____.
Sophie:	What do you recommend? I'm a vegetarian, but I ⁴_____ eat fish.
Jack:	Then you should get the ⁵_____ fish special. It's really delicious.
Yuya:	What's the ⁶_____ between the A-set and the B-set?
Jack:	The *tonkatsu* is bigger in the B-set, so it's a little more expensive. It also comes with a drink and dessert. You can have as ⁷_____ ⁸_____ and shredded cabbage as you want in both sets.
Kaira:	I'm not so hungry so I'll have the A-set.
Yuya:	Do you get ⁹_____ soon, Jack? We're thinking of going to karaoke after dinner. Mai and Angelo are going to join us later.
Jack:	I work until 10:00, but I can meet you ¹⁰_____.

▶ Now complete what Sophie and Kaira will probably order.

```
Sophie
Daily (              )
  → She is a (              )
  but sometimes eats (          ).
```

```
Kaira
(      )-set
  → She is not so (              ).
```

❷ Using the expressions you have learned so far, fill in the blanks and then practice these three mini-conversations with your partner.

1. A: What do you _____? I'm a vegetarian.

　　B: Then you _____ _____ the bean curry. It's really _____.

2. A: What's the difference _____ the A-set and B-set?

　　B: Drinks and salads are included in the B-set.

3. A: If you order this, you can have as much rice and salad as you want.

　　B: I'm not so _____ so I'll just have soup.

50

Conversation B The international club members are talking about the food they will bring to Jack's dinner party.

❶ Listen to their conversation and complete the two key sentences.

Conversation 🎧 DL 45 🔘 CD2-05 **Key Sentences** 🎧 DL 46 🔘 CD2-06

Mai:	What are you bringing to Jack's international dinner party, Angelo?
Angelo:	A Filipino stew called *adobo*. It's made with chicken or pork …
Kaira:	Well, I'm bringing *samosas*.
Mai:	Is that a kind of curry?
Kaira:	No. They are bite-sized appetizers made with spicy potatoes that are wrapped in a crust and deep-fried. They're a little like *gyoza*.
Sophie:	I don't have time to cook, so I'm bringing California wine.
Mai:	I'm making *temaki* sushi. 🔑1 **It's** _____ (4) to make. **It's** _____ (5).
Sophie:	I wonder if Jack will make something Australian.
Mai:	He told me he ordered kangaroo meat from an online shop.
Everyone:	Kangaroo!
Mai:	Yeah. 🔑2 **He said** _____ _____ (7), healthy, and natural. He wants us to try it!

❷ Take turns being A and B and practice this conversation with your partner. You can choose expressions from the hints or think of your own.

A: What are you bringing to our potluck party?

B: Well, I'm going to { make / bring }   a .

A: Is that a kind of   b ?

B: { Yes / No / Kind of } { They are / It is }   c . How about you? What will you make?

A: I'm { making / bringing }   *your idea* .

Hints
-ˈöˈ-

a	tacos / pad thai / okonomiyaki
b	sandwich / noodle dish / Japanese dish
c	Mexican food made with tortillas and a filling / stir fried noodles with vegetables and meat / a Japanese pancake containing cabbage and meat or seafood

Expressing Yourself

Your Opinion Express your own view by answering the following question. Review the key sentences you learned on the previous page, if you like.

❓ Question

> What kind of Japanese food do you think your foreign friends should try? Describe the food.

—I recommend _____

The food is _____

Writing a Recipe Imagine a foreign friend wants to learn how to make a simple and easy Japanese dinner. You recommend curry and rice.

▶ First, choose the ingredients for your curry below:

- Meat   { chicken beef pork seafood other _____ }
- Vegetables { potatoes carrots green beans pumpkin other _____ }
- Side dish   { sliced tomatoes green salad other _____ }

▶ Next, write the recipe.

● How to Make Curry and Rice ●

It is very easy to make curry and rice. Anyone can make it!

First, cut the _____ into bite-sized pieces. Add oil to the pan and fry it. While the _____ is frying, cut the vegetables. I usually use _____, _____, _____, and _____.

Put water in the pan and add the vegetables. When everything is cooked, add the curry roux.

Curry and rice is good served with _____.

I hope you enjoy the dish!

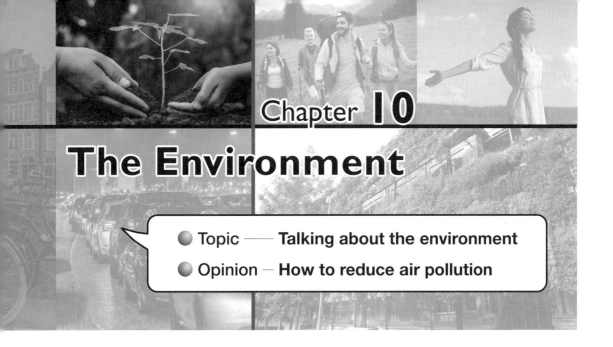

Chapter 10

The Environment

- Topic —— **Talking about the environment**
- Opinion — **How to reduce air pollution**

Breaking the Ice

Fill in the blanks with your information, and then practice asking and answering the questions with your partner.   DL 47   CD2-07

1. When you go shopping, do you usually bring your own bag or use the store's plastic bag?

—I usually _____ when I go shopping.

2. Which do you use more often, public transportation or your bicycle?

—I use _____ more often.

3. Which of these do you recycle: paper, plastic, or clothes?

—I recycle _____.

4. What do you think is a more serious environmental problem, air pollution or water pollution?

—I think _____ is more serious.

Getting the Topic

Vocabulary Matching Match each word or expression with its meaning.

1. proposal   ·   · **a.** to make air, water, or other things dirty
2. religious   ·   · **b.** a person working to achieve an ideal
3. pollute   ·   · **c.** when a plant or animal has died out completely
4. extinction ·   · **d.** an idea or suggestion
5. activist   ·   · **e.** believing in a god

Earth Day

In the 1950s and 1960s, a scientist and peace activist named John McConnell became increasingly worried about the earth. He thought that humans were not taking care of the environment. He proposed a special holiday to educate people about environmental issues. His

5

proposal won support from many politicians, and the first Earth Day was held in March 1970. Universities and schools around the United States held 10 activities to make people think about environmental problems such as pollution, oil spills, and wildlife extinction.

Nowadays, Earth Day is celebrated in 190 countries on April 22. More than a billion people take part in Earth Day activities, making it the biggest non-religious celebration in the world. Human rights and peace activists 15 want people to change their behavior so everyone can enjoy the planet's natural resources for centuries to come. One of the most common Earth Day activities is to plant trees. Trees can improve the environment by reducing greenhouse gasses, producing oxygen, providing homes for birds and insects, and controlling pollution. The year 2020 marks the 50th anniversary of 20 Earth Day. Isn't that wonderful?

True or False | Answer if the statement is true or false.

1. John McConnell believed people did not take good care of the earth. [T / F]

2. Earth Day is celebrated in 300 countries on April 22. [T / F]

3. Earth Day has become an important religious holiday. [T / F]

4. The 50th anniversary of Earth Day is in 2020. [T / F]

Speaking Up

Conversation A Mai and Angelo are talking about climbing Mt. Fuji.

❶ Listen to their conversation and fill in the blanks. Then practice it with your partner.   🎧 DL 49 ◎ CD2-09

Mai: Our club members are going to climb Mt. Fuji this summer. Do you want to come with us?

Angelo: I ¹_____ do! Climbing Mt. Fuji is number one on my list of things ²_____ ³_____ in Japan.

Mai: Great! Can you help me ⁴_____ an email? I want to ⁵_____ people know the date, time, and rules.

Angelo: Rules?

Mai: Yeah. For example, damaging plants, ⁶_____ animals, and taking ⁷_____ any stones are prohibited.

Angelo: That's common ⁸_____, isn't it?

Mai: Yeah, but I remember a ⁹_____ I saw at a national park in Australia. It said, "Take a picture, leave a memory."

Angelo: Hmm? Oh! I get it. Don't *take away anything*. Just "take a picture." And don't *leave anything behind* like trash. Just "leave a memory."

Mai: I want to ¹⁰_____ that slogan to the email!

▶ Now complete the meaning of the slogan.

> Take a picture = Don't (   )
> Leave a memory = Don't (   )

❷ Using the expressions you have learned so far, fill in the blanks and then practice these three mini-conversations with your partner.

1. **A:** My brother and I are thinking of visiting Yakushima this _____.
   Do you _____ to come with us?
   B: I _____ do!

2. **A:** Climbing Mt. McKinley is on my _____ of things to do in the U.S.
   B: How cool!

3. **A:** Can you _____ me write an email?
   B: Sure! I'd be happy to help.

Conversation B Yuya and Kaira are hanging around in Ginza one Saturday afternoon.

❶ Listen to their conversation and complete the two key sentences.

Conversation 🎧 DL 50 ⊙ CD2-10 **Key Sentences** 🎧 DL 51 ⊙ CD2-11

Kaira: It's nice to be able to walk in the middle of the main street in Ginza!

Yuya: It really is. An Earth Day event several decades ago led to the idea of *hokosha-tengoku*, or pedestrian zones.

Kaira: 💡1 _____

_____ (9). In Delhi it's terrible. About 10,000 people die every year because of pollution.

Yuya: Well, the pollution in Tokyo used to be terrible. They started to clean it up in the 1970s.

Kaira: 💡2 _____ (6) **policy**. Cars with license plates ending in odd numbers like 1 or 3 and cars with license plates ending in even numbers like 2 or 4 drive on alternate days.

Yuya: Does that help reduce pollution?

Kaira: Yes—to some extent. But we need to do more.

❷ Take turns being A and B and practice this conversation with your partner. You can choose expressions from the hints or think of your own.

A: I can't believe how clean this ▓ a ▓ is now.

B: Really? What was it like before?

A: People used to ▓ b ▓. It was terrible.

B: What caused the change?

A: After an Earth Day event a few years ago, people started ▓ c ▓.

Hints
🔅

a	beach / river / park
b	litter everywhere / dump trash into the river / smoke on the streets
c	disposing of trash properly / taking their garbage home / a no-smoking campaign

Expressing Yourself

Your Opinion Express your own view by answering the following question. Review the key sentences you learned on the previous page, if you like.

❓ Question

Air pollution is a serious environmental problem around the world. What do you think we can do to reduce air pollution? Or if you know about any measure that has been already taken somewhere, explain it.

—I think we can _____

—My town started _____

—According to a news article, in _____ , they _____

Writing an Announcement Imagine you are going to hold an Earth Day event. Make a poster to let people know about the event.

▶ First, fill in the following information.

- Location _____

- Main activity _____

  (plant trees, make a community garden, pick up trash, go on a short bicycle trip, meet with local people, etc.)

- Other features _____

  (speeches by experts, vegetarian lunches, live music all day, etc.)

▶ Next, complete a poster so everyone can learn about your event.

> *Join us for Our Earth Day Celebration!*
>
> *Spend the day in _____ celebrating Mother Earth!*
> *We are going to _____ .*
> *The festival also includes _____ .*
>
> *More to be announced!*

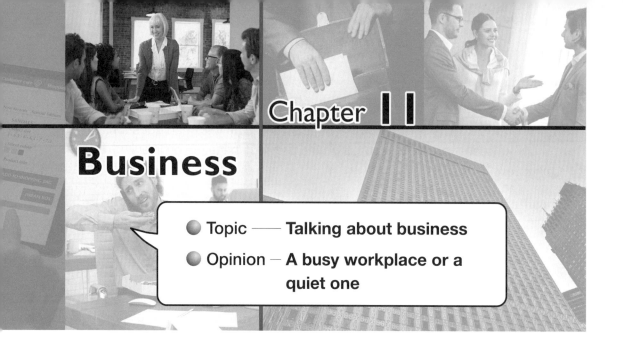

Chapter 11

Business

- Topic —— **Talking about business**
- Opinion – **A busy workplace or a quiet one**

Breaking the Ice

Fill in the blanks with your information, and then practice asking and answering the questions with your partner. DL 52 CD2-12

1. Do you want to work for a company or start your own business in the future?

　—I want to ＿＿＿＿＿＿＿＿＿＿＿＿＿＿＿ in the future.

2. Which is more secure, working for a large company or a small company?

　—I think it's more secure to ＿＿＿＿＿＿＿＿＿＿＿＿＿＿＿.

3. Will English be important or unimportant for you in your future job?

　—It will ＿＿＿＿＿＿＿＿＿＿ in my future job.

4. Which industry sounds the most interesting to you: entertainment, food, publishing, or manufacturing?

　—The ＿＿＿＿＿＿＿＿＿＿＿＿＿＿＿ sounds the most interesting to me.

Getting the Topic

Vocabulary Matching Match each word or expression with its meaning.

1. distance · · **a.** to check for information
2. essential · · **b.** stated directly
3. lose its appeal · · **c.** the space between two points
4. refer to · · **d.** necessary
5. to the point · · **e.** not as popular as it used to be

Reading Read the passage for information.

SMS and email

Technology has made it possible for people to communicate easily with others regardless of time and distance. In 2017, nearly 30 trillion text messages were sent worldwide, and that mode of communication has become far more popular than email. Email, widely popular in the 1990s,  lost its appeal among young people because of spam and computer viruses, and they think it is a formal way to communicate. Nonetheless, both texting and emailing are essential, particularly in business communication.

SMS messages, or text messages, are sent to personal smartphones, so the senders are people you already know. Messages are received instantly, and this is useful in urgent situations. They are short and get right to the point. However, the senders often expect quick replies. This might be bothersome, especially when messages are business related and arrive outside of working hours.

Email messages are generally more formal and longer than texts, and they often have attached documents. Importantly, a record of the correspondence between the sender and receiver is made. Such records are essential in business because they can be referred to at any time.

True or False Answer if the statement is true or false.

1. Sending email is as popular as it used to be.   [T / F]
2. Business communication only uses email.   [T / F]
3. Text messages tend to be more formal than emails.   [T / F]
4. An advantage of email is that messages can be saved easily and looked at
   again at any time.   [T / F]

Speaking Up

Conversation A Kaira and Mai are talking about women entrepreneurs.

❶ Listen to their conversation and fill in the blanks. Next, practice it with your partner.
　　　　　　　　　　　　　　　　　　　　　　🎧 DL 54　◉ CD2-14

Mai: You're eating a Japanese *obento* ¹_____! I guess you can't buy Japanese food in India.

Kaira: Actually, ²_____ a lot. In fact, my sister imports Japanese food. She has her own e-commerce business.

Mai: She's an entrepreneur? How ³_____!

Kaira: Online shopping is really popular, and there are many successful women in this field now. I want to start my ⁴_____ ⁵_____, too.

Mai: That sounds great, but someday I want to get ⁶_____.

Kaira: You can do ⁷_____. My sister is married and has three ⁸_____.

Mai: I don't want to run a business. I'd like to work for an ⁹_____ company. Maybe I'll work for your company ¹⁰_____!

▶ Now complete the following information.

Kaira's sister
Owns her own (　　　　　　)
→ The company (　　　　　　)
Japanese food

Mai's future plans
● Get (　　　　　　　　)
● May work for (　　　　　　) someday

❷ Using the expressions you have learned so far, fill in the blanks and then practice these three mini-conversations with your partner.

1. A: My friend has her own e-commerce business. She imports Finnish products to Japan.
　　B: She's an _____? How _____!

2. A: I want to _____ my _____ business.
　　B: That's great!

3. A: I don't want to _____ a _____. I want to _____ married and have children.
　　B: Don't say that. You can do both.

Conversation B Yuya, Sophie, Angelo, and Jack are talking about what they want to do in the future.

❶ Listen to their conversation and complete the two key sentences.

Conversation 🎧 DL 55   ⊙ CD2-15   **Key Sentences** 🎧 DL 56   ⊙ CD2-16

Yuya: Last summer I really enjoyed interning at an American IT company.

Sophie: What was the company like?

Yuya: 🔑1 **The employees were so busy. Everyone** _____

_____ (9).

Angelo: It must be difficult to get a lot of work done when you always have to be online.

Sophie: I'd hate that job. I don't like being disturbed when I'm working.

Jack: That's because you want to be a translator. Translators need a quiet place to work.

Sophie: True. So Yuya, where do you want to work after you graduate?

Yuya: I'm not sure. 🔑2 **I want to** _____

_____ (11) English.

Sophie: Maybe you'll find a job that will send you to America.

Yuya: Wouldn't that be fantastic!

❷ Take turns being A and B and practice this conversation with your partner. You can choose expressions from the hints or think of your own.

A: I { enjoyed / hated } interning at ⬛ a ⬛ last month.

B: What was the ⬛ a ⬛ like?

A: The employees were ⬛ b ⬛ .

B: It must be ⬛ c ⬛ to ⬛ d ⬛ . So where do you want to work after you graduate?

B: I'm not sure, but. I want to work for a company where I can ⬛ e ⬛ .

Hints

a	a hospital / a trading company / a hotel
b	kind and friendly / always busy / mean to the interns
c	great / hard / fun
d	work with people like that / learn a lot of new things / meet customers
e	use my management skills / grow professionally

Expressing Yourself

Your Opinion Express your own view by answering the following questions. Review the key sentences you learned on the previous page, if you like.

❓ Questions

> In the future, what kind of company do you want to work for? Do you prefer a busy workplace or a quiet one? Why?

—I want to work for _____

because _____

Writing an Email Imagine you are job hunting. You want to ask someone who graduated from your university about a job you are interested in.

▶ First, choose an industry you are interested in and things about a job that are important to you.

- Industry _____
  (publishing, entertainment, food, IT, financial, public sector, etc.)
- Important things for you
  - salary   { age based / performance based }
  - working hours   { long / fixed / flexible }
  - working environment { creative / stable / stimulating / not so busy /
                          friendly / other _____ }

▶ Next, write to a friend who graduated last year and works in that industry. Ask questions about his/her job.

○○○

Dear _____ ,

How are you? I am interested in working in the _____
industry.   May I ask you some questions about your job?
First, is the salary _____ ?
Second, are the working hours _____ ?
Finally, is your working environment _____ ?
Thank you in advance.

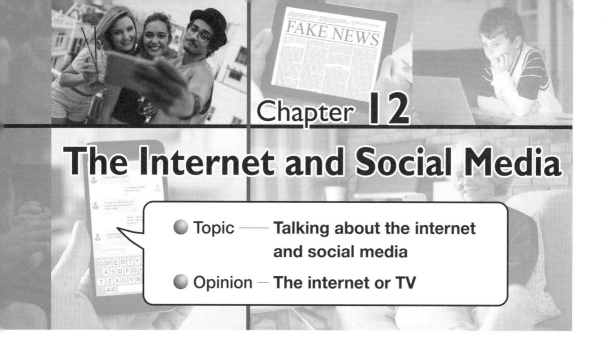

Chapter **12**

The Internet and Social Media

● Topic —— **Talking about the internet and social media**

● Opinion — **The internet or TV**

Breaking the Ice

Fill in the blanks with your information, and then practice asking and answering the questions with your partner.   🎧 DL 57   ⊙ CD2-17

1. How many hours a day do you usually use your phone?
   —I usually use my phone for about _____ a day.
2. Which social media sites do you use the most: Facebook, Twitter, Instagram, or another site?
   —I use _____ the most.
3. Where do you get information when you have to write a report: the library, the internet, or another source?
   —I often get information from _____.
4. Which type of news do you prefer reading about: celebrity news, weather news, domestic news, or international news?
   —I prefer reading about _____.

Getting the Topic

Vocabulary Matching Match each word or expression with its meaning.

1. fake ·   · **a.** a person who studies stars
2. rumor ·   · **b.** not real or truthful
3. replace ·   · **c.** to reach or cover a wide area
4. astronomer ·   · **d.** substitute
5. spread ·   · **e.** a story that may not be true

Reading Read the passage for information.

Fake news

 DL 58 CD2-18

Fake news is not a new problem. In 1835, a newspaper in New York reported that an English astronomer had discovered life on the moon. It said that he had a new telescope, and through it, he could see many living things, such as a unicorn and other strange creatures. A few weeks later,  5 however, the newspaper said that they had made the story up.

Anyone can write anything and post it on the internet. On one hand, this 10 is good. We can communicate with friends and keep up with current events. On the other hand, we have to be careful not to believe everything we read. For example, there was an old rumor in the 1960s that former Beatle Paul McCartney had died and was replaced by someone who looked just like him. That story recently appeared again on the internet! Of course, it is still 15 untrue. We have to be careful not to spread fake news. After a strong earthquake in Osaka in 2018, there was a Twitter message saying that a zebra had escaped from the zoo there. That message was retweeted hundreds of times even though it never happened!

True or False Answer if the statement is true or false.

1. Fake news is a recent problem.   [T / F]
2. Paul McCartney died in the 1960s.   [T / F]
3. One example of fake news reported life on the moon.   [T / F]
4. A lion escaped from a Japanese zoo after an earthquake. [T / F]

Speaking Up

Conversation A Sophie and Angelo are talking about a problem that happened in Sophie's class.

❶ Listen to their conversation and fill in the blanks. Next, practice it with your partner. DL 59 CD2-19

Sophie: There was a big problem in Professor Evans' ¹_____. One of the students copied and ²_____ her report from the internet.

Angelo: That's terrible! What did the professor do?

Sophie: She failed the student. But that ³_____ the ⁴_____ problem.

Angelo: What ⁵_____ happened? Did someone else plagiarize?

Sophie: No, but some students used ⁶_____ ⁷_____ for their papers.

Angelo: What do you mean?

Sophie: Some reports had fake information in them. So Professor Evans gave us a new ⁸_____ : How to Use the Internet Wisely.

Angelo: Well, that ⁹_____ like a pretty useful topic. It's important to know these things, ¹⁰_____ after we start working.

▶ Now complete what happened in Professor Evens' class.

- A student (   ) her report from the internet.
- Some students (   ) for their papers.
- → Professor's new assignment: (   )

❷ Using the expressions you have learned so far, fill in the blanks and then practice these three mini-conversations with your partner.

1. **A:** There was a big _____ at school. One of the students used his smartphone during an exam.
   B: That's _____!
2. **A:** What did the professor do?
   B: She _____ the student.
3. **A:** Professor Kato gave us an _____ : How to Use Your Smartphone Wisely.
   B: Well, that seems _____ a pretty _____ topic.

Conversation B Sophie, Kaira, Jack, and Yuya are talking about internet news.

❶ Listen to their conversation and complete the two key sentences.

Conversation 🎧 DL 60 ⊙ CD2-20 Key Sentences 🎧 DL 61 ⊙ CD2-21

Sophie: Jack, we're having dinner now. Please put away your phone.

Kaira: Come on, Jack. Admit it. You're addicted to your smartphone.

Jack: I know I use it too much, but there are so many interesting articles to read.

Yuya: Yeah, but there's also a lot of misinformation on the internet as well.
💬1 **It's** _____ (9).

Kaira: I disagree. 💬2 **As long as** _____
_____ (11).

Sophie: I like the internet, but I also watch TV news shows because the commentators have unique views on current events. They help me learn a lot about Japan.

Kaira: What's important is to know that not all news is real news.

Sophie: Absolutely! If something sounds too crazy to be true, it probably isn't true.

❷ Take turns being A and B and practice this conversation with your partner. You can choose expressions from the hints or think of your own.

A: _name_ , please put away your phone. I think you have an addiction!

B: I know I use it too much, but   a .

A: I know there is a lot of   b   information on the internet as well, but there's also a lot of   c .

B: True. It is really important to   d   when using the internet.

Hints
- -

a	I can't stop tweeting / I like being online / I learn a lot from blogs
b	useful / interesting / important
c	fake news / dangerous information / biased information
d	be careful / think carefully / check the source of information

Expressing Yourself

Your Opinion Express your own view by answering the following questions. Review the key sentences you learned on the previous page, if you like.

❓ Questions

> Where do you usually get information about current events: the internet or TV? What are their advantages?

—I often get information from TV news programs because _____

_____

—My favorite TV news program is _____

_____

—I get my news online more often. The internet is useful because _____

_____

Writing Text Messages Imagine you saw a funny story on the internet and want to tell a friend about it.

▶ First, read the text message and guess the meaning of the abbreviations in bold.

> **TQ** for helping me **2nte**! Your advice was **GR8**.
> **BTW**, I just saw something funny on the Internet. Students at XYZ University can bring their pets to class now! But the university said it was fake news! **LOL**
> Anyway, **CU** tomorrow. **XOXOXO**

- TQ = (   )   · 2nte = (   )
- GR8 = (   )   · BTW = (   )
- LOL = (   )   · CU = (   )
- XOXOXO = (   )

▶ Next, write a text message to your friend about a funny story. Try to use some of the abbreviations above.

_____

_____

_____

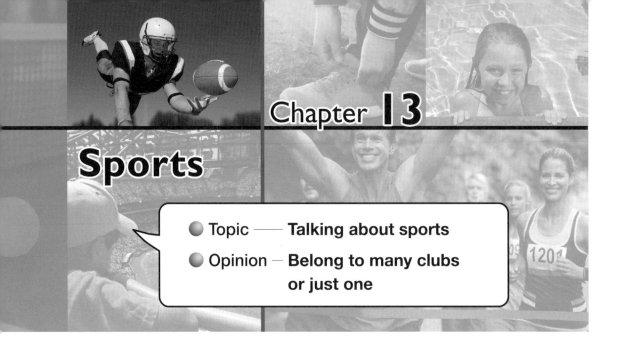

Chapter 13

Sports

- Topic —— **Talking about sports**
- Opinion – **Belong to many clubs or just one**

Breaking the Ice

Fill in the blanks with your information, and then practice asking and answering the questions with your partner. DL 62   CD2-22

1. Which sport is more popular in Japan, baseball or soccer?

—I think _____ is more popular.

2. In high school, were you in a sports club or a non-athletic club?

—I was in a _____.

3. Which do you enjoy more, team sports or individual sports?

—I enjoy _____ more.

4. Do you prefer to watch sports or play sports?

—I prefer _____.

Getting the Topic

Vocabulary Matching Match each word or expression with its meaning.

1. spectators ·   · **a.** to sign up for
2. register   ·   · **b.** a person in charge
3. an official ·   · **c.** to protest against
4. disqualify ·   · **d.** to not be allowed to do something
5. object to   ·   · **e.** people who watch an event

Reading Read the passage for information.

First woman to run in the Boston Marathon

The Boston Marathon started in 1897 with just fifteen runners, but now 30,000 amateurs and professionals run before 500,000 spectators. Nowadays nearly 50% of the participants are female, but this was not always so. In fact, women were not allowed to enter the race until 1972.

Kathy Switzer registered for the race in 1967 under the name K.V. Switzer. 10
The organizers thought she was a man, and she was given an official bib with the number 261. After Kathy had run for four miles, a marathon official realized that K.V. Switzer was a woman. Photojournalists captured the moment when he tried to push her off the course and take her bib. Several people tried to stop him and Kathy was able to reach the finish line. 15
However, she was disqualified from the competition because the organizers objected to a woman competing with men. Five years later, however, the rules changed. Kathy was recognized as a hero because she had broken gender barriers. Nowadays, the number 261 is not assigned to any other runner in recognition of Kathy Switzer's contribution to women in sports. 20

True or False Answer if the statement is true or false.

1. The Boston Marathon started with 50 runners. [T / F]

2. Women were allowed to participate in the Boston Marathon
before 1972. [T / F]

3. Officials first thought Kathy was a man. [T / F]

4. Nowadays about half of the Boston Marathon runners are female. [T / F]

Speaking Up

Conversation A Kaira and Angelo are talking about running in the Tokyo Marathon.

❶ Listen to their conversation and fill in the blanks. Next, practice it with your partner.   🎧 DL 64   ⊙ CD2-24

Angelo: Are you going to run in the Tokyo Marathon?

Kaira: Yeah! ¹_____ ²_____ marathons in India and Europe. I really want to run in Japan, too.

Angelo: Do you think you can ³_____ the race?

Kaira: Of course ⁴_____! The winners are world famous champions. I just want to finish!

Angelo: How many runners can take ⁵_____?

Kaira: The maximum is 37,000. There were so many ⁶_____ they had a lottery. I was lucky I got ⁷_____.

Angelo: Aren't there any requirements?

Kaira: You have to be able to complete the course in ⁸_____ seven hours.

Angelo: That's hard! Do you know the gender proportion of the runners?

Kaira: Yes. Nowadays ⁹_____ ¹⁰_____ more than 20% are women. But that number will increase every year!

▶ Now complete the facts about the Tokyo Marathon.

Maximum number of runners: (   )
Requirement: Able to (   )
Approximate gender proportion: Male (   )% / Female (   )%

❷ Using the expressions you have learned so far, fill in the blanks and then practice these three mini-conversations with your partner.

1. **A:** Are you _____ to take part in the company's sports event?
   B: Yeah! I couldn't last year, so I _____ _____ to do it this year.

2. **A:** Do you think you can _____ first prize?
   B: Of course _____!

3. **A:** People participating in the marathon have to _____ _____ to run 10 kilometers in one hour.
   B: That's _____!

Conversation B Sophie and Yuya are talking about the sports they played in high school.

❶ Listen to their conversation and complete the two key sentences.

Conversation 🎧 DL 65 ⊙ CD2-25   **Key Sentences** 🎧 DL 66 ⊙ CD2-26

Sophie: I'm really getting out of shape.

Yuya: You look fine to me.

Sophie: Do you want to go jogging together after school sometime?

Yuya: Jogging? Sure. Were you in the track and field club in high school?

Sophie: Yes. I also was on the tennis team and the swim team. What sports did you play?

Yuya: I was in the table tennis club for six years. It was really fun.

Sophie: Oh yeah. 🔑1 _____ (8).

Yuya: What about in America?

Sophie: 🔑2 **We can** _____ (9).

My brother played football in the fall, basketball in the winter, and baseball in the spring. He was also on the swim team in the summer.

Yuya: Wow! That sounds so busy! I'm not sure which is better—playing many sports or just one!

❷ Take turns being A and B and practice this conversation with your partner. You can choose expressions from the hints or think of your own.

A: I need to get in shape.

B: Do you a ? I used to do that when I was b . I was in the c club.

A: You were so athletic! I'm not good at sports. I prefer to d .

B: Sports are not only important for our health, but they are also e .

Hints

a	play tennis / run / swim
b	in elementary school / in junior high / in high school
c	tennis / swimming / track and field
d	take photos / play the piano / draw pictures
e	fun / challenging / exciting

Expressing Yourself

Your Opinion Express your own view by answering the following question. Review the key sentences you learned on the previous page, if you like.

❓ Question

> Which do you think is better, belonging to many clubs or just one?

—I think belonging to one club is better. When I was in high school, _____

_____

—Belonging to many clubs is good because _____

Writing Text Messages Imagine you are texting your friend about going to the university gym this weekend.

▶ First, check what you want to do at the gym.

☐ use the weight machines   ☐ use the swimming pool   ☐ run on the treadmill
☐ practice in the *dojo*   ☐ play on the basketball court   ☐ relax in the sauna
☐ do yoga   ☐ other _____

▶ Next, underline what you think your friend might be interested in from the above and complete the text messages.

(You   )
Hi _____.
Are you free this weekend? Let's go to the university gym.

(Your friend   )
Hi. I'm not busy. But I don't do sports.

(You   )
Come on! There are a lot of great facilities there!
I'm going to _____.

(Your friend   )
Sounds good, but I'm not really interested in _____.

(Your name   )
Then, why don't you _____ while I'm _____?
There's a/an _____ in the gym!

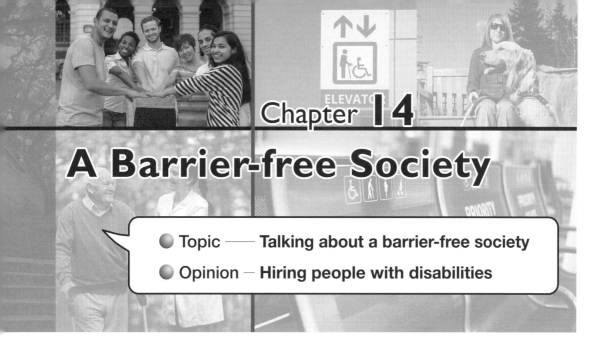

Chapter **14**

A Barrier-free Society

> ● Topic —— **Talking about a barrier-free society**
> ● Opinion — **Hiring people with disabilities**

Breaking the Ice

Fill in the blanks with your information, and then practice asking and answering the questions with your partner. 🎧 DL 67 ⦿ CD2-27

1. Is it easy or hard for people with disabilities to get around your campus?
    —It is _____ for them.
2. Do you continue to sit or do you stand up if you see someone with physical difficulties on the train?
    —I usually _____.
3. Which places in Japan might be challenging for people with disabilities to visit: temples and shrines, train stations, or museums?
    —I think _____ might be challenging.
4. Which have you seen recently: sign language interpreting on TV, wheelchair-accessible restrooms, or service dogs?
    —I have seen _____.

Getting the Topic

Vocabulary Matching | Match each word or expression with its meaning.

1. deaf   · · **a.** money problems
2. determined   · · **b.** the results are very satisfying
3. financial difficulties · · **c.** cannot hear
4. rewarding   · · **d.** rising or falling rapidly
5. steep   · · **e.** wanting to do something very much

No limitations!

DL 68   CD2-28

Suzanne Kamata is an American writer living in Shikoku. She writes novels, short stories, non-fiction essays, and memoirs. Her recent memoir, *Squeaky Wheels*, describes her travels with her daughter. Lilia is deaf and uses a wheelchair. Nonetheless, Lilia wanted to see the world. Suzanne was determined to make her daughter's dream come true. They went to Naoshima Island in Japan, where they slept in a museum. They traveled to the American state of Tennessee, where they explored caves. They visited major cities such as Washington, D.C. and New York. Lilia's dream was to see Paris, and despite financial and practical difficulties, Suzanne made that happen.

Suzanne and Lilia

Suzanne writes that travelling with her daughter is extremely rewarding, 15 but it is also full of challenges. When they visit unfamiliar places, they don't know if there will be a ramp for wheelchairs. Sometimes Suzanne has to push her daughter's manual wheelchair up steep hills. Despite the difficulties, Suzanne and Lilia have had many interesting adventures. However, now that Lilia is getting older, she may not want to travel with her 20 mother. She may want to travel with her friends instead!

True or False Answer if the statement is true or false.

1. Suzanne Kamata is a British writer living in Japan.　　　　[T / F]

2. Lilia's dream to travel the world did not come true.　　　　[T / F]

3. It's possible to travel around the world in a wheelchair.　　　[T / F]

4. Lilia may now want to travel with her friends more than
　　with her mother.　　　　　　　　　　　　　　　　　[T / F]

Speaking Up

Conversation A Mai and Yuya are talking about where to have a party after the International Student Speech Contest.

❶ Listen to their conversation and fill in the blanks. Next, practice it with your partner. 🎧 DL 69 ⊙ CD2-29

Mai: Do you know of a good place to ¹_____ our party?

Yuya: Well, there's a cheap place near campus ²_____ the food is delicious. It's small, so we can reserve the ³_____ restaurant.

Mai: Is there an elevator? Hans Weber is ⁴_____ ⁵_____ the contestants, and he uses a ⁶_____ .

Yuya: No, there's no elevator. And I just remembered something. Jack sprained his ⁷_____ in karate class. I wonder if he's all right now.

Mai: He said he needs to use crutches for a few weeks.

Yuya: All right. We need to ⁸_____ looking. The party venue needs to be ⁹_____ . Anything else?

Mai: Yes. We need to find a restaurant that doesn't ¹⁰_____ pork for our Muslim participants.

▶ Now complete what the ideal party venue is like.

- Cheap and located (   )
- Has an (   )
- Doesn't serve (   )

❷ Using the expressions you have learned so far, fill in the blanks and then practice these three mini-conversations with your partner.

1. A: Do you know of a good _____ to hold the party?
   B: There's a cheap place near here.
2. A: Is there an _____?
   B: I'll check. That's important because one of our _____ uses a _____.
3. A: We need to find a restaurant that doesn't serve pork.
   B: That's right. We have some _____ participants.

❶ Listen to their conversation and complete the two key sentences.

Conversation 🎧 DL 70 💿 CD2-30   **Key Sentences** 🎧 DL 71 💿 CD2-31

Yuya: Congratulations! You won the speech contest.

Hans: Thanks. I'm really glad that so many people liked my speech.

Yuya: Your topic was really eye-opening! I've never thought about how difficult it might be for people with disabilities to get a job.

Hans: That's because people often make wrong assumptions. 🔑1 **They believe people like me** _____ (9). Just because I can't walk doesn't mean I can't be a good employee.

Yuya: So what kind of work do you want to do after you graduate?

Hans: I want to work for a manufacturing company. I'd like to stay in Japan, but it might be hard to find a job here.

Yuya: 🔑2 **I think** _____ _____ (7). I believe companies can benefit a lot from a diverse workforce.

❷ Take turns being A and B and practice this conversation with your partner. You can choose expressions from the hints or think of your own.

A: ▨ *name of workplace you work part time* ▨ is going to hire a woman who is ▨ a ▨ .

B: Really? Won't it be difficult for her to work if she can't ▨ b ▨ ?

A: Maybe. But our manager says she is very skilled. She's good at ▨ c ▨ and ▨ c ▨ .

B: It sounds like we can probably learn a lot from her. And we can always ▨ d ▨ if she has trouble with anything.

(Hints)
- a blind / deaf / in a wheelchair
- b see / hear / walk
- c making sweets / selling things / using computers / speaking English / organizing people
- d support her / offer help / encourage her

Expressing Yourself

Your Opinion Express your own view by answering the following question. Review the key sentences you learned on the previous page, if you like.

❓ Question

> Japanese companies will probably hire more people with disabilities in the future. What are the benefits of having this kind of diversity?

—I think people with disabilities can benefit from working because _____

_____

—I think companies can benefit because _____

_____

Writing an Email Imagine you are going to visit a museum with members of the International Student Association. Write an email to the museum asking about its accessibility.

▶ First, decide what type of museum you want to visit, and then check what the members of your group need.

Type of museum _____ (art, science, manga, open-air, etc.)
☐ wheelchair ramps ☐ Braille guidebooks ☐ elevators to all floors
☐ accessible restrooms ☐ multilingual announcements
☐ easy access to the building ☐ nearby parking ☐ student discounts

▶ Next, write an email to the museum.

Hello,
I am a student from _____ University. Our International Student Association will visit _____ in _____. We have some students with disabilities, so I would like to confirm your museum has the necessary facilities. First, do you have _____?
We also need _____. Thank you for your time.

Sincerely,

_____

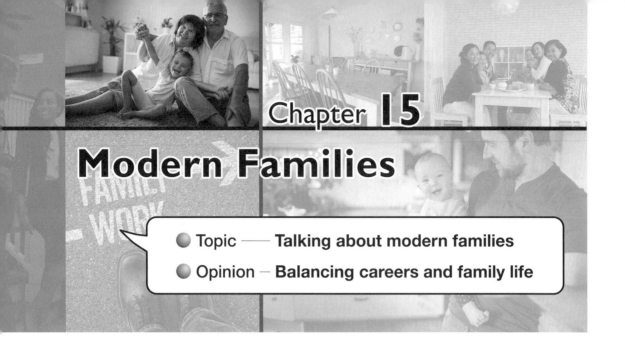

Chapter 15

Modern Families

- ● Topic —— **Talking about modern families**
- ● Opinion — **Balancing careers and family life**

Breaking the Ice

Fill in the blanks with your information, and then practice asking and answering the
questions with your partner. DL 72 CD2-32

1. How many people are there in your family?
   —There are _____ .
2. Did you live near or far from your grandparents when you were a child?
   —I lived _____ .
3. Do you think families will become larger or smaller in the future?
   —I think families will become _____ .
4. Do you eat with your family regularly or only on special occasions?
   —I eat with my family _____ .

Getting the Topic

Vocabulary Matching Match each word or expression with its meaning.

1. extended family ·		· **a.** to speak to someone for the first time
2. spouse ·		· **b.** great success
3. triumph ·		· **c.** to give support and advice
4. approach ·		· **d.** a family living together with grandparents
5. encourage ·		· **e.** a person someone is married to

Reading Read the passage for information.

21st century families

Humans traditionally lived in extended families with spouses and in-laws. People moved to cities during the industrial era, and this resulted in the nuclear family. Family dynamics changed in the latter half of the 20th century, and divorce became common. Some children's

5

parents remarry. Then they will have a stepparent and perhaps stepbrothers or stepsisters. A new baby would be their half brother or half sister. 10

Adopting and raising a boy or a girl who is not a biological child is also becoming common. Melodie Cook, a Canadian professor living in Niigata, writes about the challenges and triumphs of being an adoptive parent in a Tokyo magazine called *Savvy*. Her column provides a lot of information for Japanese and non-Japanese who want to adopt or foster children. For 15 example, one of her articles describes the difficulties faced by an American who wanted to adopt a child in Japan. She and her Japanese husband approached many adoption agencies. They learned that even though numerous children live in institutions, few children are available for adoption. Furthermore, some agencies only consider prospective parents if 20 both parents are Japanese. It is important for couples like this to not give up their hopes. Melodie's column encourages readers to expand their perceptions of "family." In the end, a family is a group of people who love and support each other.

True or False Answer if the statement is true or false.

1. Most extended families live in cities. [T / F]
2. Divorce is now more common than it used to be. [T / F]
3. Melodie Cook has a radio program about modern society. [T / F]
4. Melodie Cook writes about adoption in Canada. [T / F]

Speaking Up

❶ Listen to their conversation and fill in the blanks. Next, practice it with your partner.　　　🎧 DL 74　💿 CD2-34

Mai: I'm going to study in California next year. The program also
¹_____ an internship I want to do. It's at an NGO that supports
²_____ care.

Jack: Why did you ³_____ to do that?

Mai: I want to work with children someday, but I don't want to be a teacher.

Jack: I heard that ⁴_____ and fostering children in Japan is
⁵_____ common than in the U.S.

Mai: Yeah, but Japanese society is changing ⁶_____ and so are
family dynamics. ⁷_____ about foster care will be important
in Japan someday.

Jack: Maybe you'll like California so much you'll decide to ⁸_____
permanently. Maybe you'll meet some guy there and get married.

Mai: I don't know about that. I'm ⁹_____ of going to
¹⁰_____ school in Australia.

▶ Now complete Mai's plans.

Next year	After college
• Study in (　　　　　)	• Go to (　　　　　)
• Do internship at (　　　　)	in Australia

❷ Using the expressions you have learned so far, fill in the blanks and then
practice these three mini-conversations with your partner.

1. A: I'm going to work at an NGO that _____ underprivileged
children.

　B: Why did you _____ to do that?

2. A: Do you want to work with _____ someday?

　B: Yes, but I don't want to be a _____.

3. A: Maybe you'll meet someone, _____ married, and stay.

　B: Actually, I was thinking of _____ to the U.K. after graduation.

Yuya is talking with the international club members about a company where he will be an intern.

❶ Listen to their conversation and complete the two key sentences.

Conversation 🎧 DL 75 ◉ CD2-35   **Key Sentences** 🎧 DL 76 ◉ CD2-36

Yuya: Guess what! I got a year-long internship at an IT startup!

Sophie: Congratulations!

Mai: It sounds like it will be a busy job.

Yuya: Yeah, but the company is innovative. Employees can work from home. So even women with children can do this job.

Sophie: That's great, but you should have put it differently: "even women" doesn't sound right.

Yuya: What do you mean?

Sophie: You should have said "people."

Jack: That's right. It's the current trend. 🔑1 _____
_____ (7).

Mai: Yeah. Husbands and wives have to balance their careers and family. Couples have to share housework and childcare.

Angelo: That's true, but it's difficult to do in reality.

Mai: 🔑2 **It doesn't matter** _____
_____ (10).

❷ Take turns being A and B and practice this conversation with your partner. You can choose expressions from the hints or think of your own.

A: Guess what! I got a year-long internship at ▸ a ◂ !

B: Congratulations! It sounds like ▸ b ◂ job. Why did you choose that company?

A: It's innovative and the employees ▸ c ◂ .

B: That's great. It will be a ▸ d ◂ .

Hints

a	a travel agency / a three-star restaurant / a research company
b	a busy / an interesting / a challenging
c	can work remotely / want to mentor interns / are enthusiastic workers
d	fantastic experience / good opportunity / great challenge

Expressing Yourself

Your Opinion | Express your own view by answering the following question. Review the key sentences you learned on the previous page, if you like.

? Question

How can husbands and wives balance careers and family life when they both work?

—Couples have to _____

—Companies have to _____

Writing Your Future Plans | Imagine a perfect life for yourself 20 years from now. Then describe your future life.

▶ First, fill in the following information.

- Type of career _____
- Where you will live _____
- Married or single _____ → Children _____
- What you do every weekend _____
- What you never want to do _____

▶ Next, complete this short paragraph to describe your future life.

● My Future Life ●

Twenty years from now, I will be _____ .

I will live in _____ { with my family / with _____ / alone }.

I { want / don't want } to be married because _____ .

{ I am / I'm not } going to have _____ children because _____

_____ .

On weekends, I will _____ .

In my future, I will never _____ . I will be very happy!

本書には CD（別売）があります

Chat and Share!
Topic Starters for Today's Students
話してみよう！ トピックベースの英会話

2020 年 1 月 20 日 初版第 1 刷発行
2024 年 3 月 10 日 初版第 9 刷発行

著　者　　Diane H. Nagatomo

発行者　　福　岡　正　人
発行所　　株式会社　金星堂

（〒101-0051）東京都千代田区神田神保町 3-21
Tel.（03）3263-3828（営業部）
（03）3263-3997（編集部）
Fax（03）3263-0716
https://www.kinsei-do.co.jp

編集担当／蔦原美智　　　　　　　　　　Printed in Japan
印刷所・製本所／三美印刷株式会社

ISBN978-4-7647-4106-5 C1082